T0059607

MY POCKET
SELF-CARE

MY POCKET
SELF-CARE

ANYTIME ACTIVITIES TO REFRESH
YOUR MIND, BODY, AND SPIRIT

ADAMS MEDIA

NEW YORK LONDON TORONTO SYDNEY NEW DELHI

Adams Media
An Imprint of Simon & Schuster, Inc.
100 Technology Center Dr.
Stoughton, Massachusetts 02072

First Adams Media trade paperback edition November 2020

ADAMS MEDIA and colophon are trademarks of Simon & Schuster.

For information about special discounts for bulk purchases, please contact Simon & Schuster Special Sales at 1-866-506-1949 or business@simonandschuster.com.

The Simon & Schuster Speakers Bureau can bring authors to your live event. For more information or to book an event contact the Simon & Schuster Speakers Bureau at 1-866-248-3049 or visit our website at www.simonspeakers.com.

Images © 123RF/Liudmila Horvath

Manufactured in China

10 9 8 7 6 5 4 3 2

Library of Congress Cataloging-in-Publication Data
Title: My pocket self-care.
Description: First Adams Media trade paperback edition. | Avon, Massachusetts: Adams Media, 2020
Series: My pocket | Includes index.
Identifiers: LCCN 2020015904 | ISBN 9781507214398 (pb) | ISBN 9781507214404 (ebook)
Subjects: LCSH: Self-care, Health--Problems, exercises, etc.
Classification: LCC RA776.95 .M9 2020 | DDC 613.076--dc23
LC record available at https://lccn.loc.gov/2020015904

ISBN 978-1-5072-1439-8
ISBN 978-1-5072-1440-4 (ebook)

Contains material adapted from the following title published by Adams Media, an Imprint of Simon & Schuster, Inc.: *Self-Care for Life* by Skye Alexander, Meera Lester, and Carolyn Dean, MD, ND, copyright © 2011, ISBN 978-1-4405-2860-6.

CONTENTS

Introduction 11

PART 1: MIND   **13**

CONSIDER HOW EMOTIONS AFFECT YOUR DECISIONS 14

ORGANIZE GOALS INTO STEPS 15

TRACK NEGATIVE THOUGHTS 16

CREATE A PERSONAL MISSION STATEMENT 17

CEASE MULTITASKING 18

ESTABLISH PERSONAL BOUNDARIES 19

REFOCUS WITH DHARANA 20

NOURISH A HIDDEN TALENT 21

FIND OPPORTUNITIES IN DELAYS 22

RECONSIDER YOUR PRIORITIES 23

IMPROVE YOUR VOCABULARY 24

JOIN A SOCIAL CLUB 25

BALANCE YOUR MINDSET WITH GINSENG 26

FOCUS ON FORGIVENESS 27

MIST YOUR CAR WITH LAVENDER 28

DETOX WITH MUDRAS 29

REVEAL YOUR FEELINGS 30

WRITE A HAIKU 31

SHIFT YOUR ATTENTION AWAY FROM YOURSELF 32

HIDE A LOVE NOTE FOR SOMEONE SPECIAL 33

PICK YOUR BATTLES 34

TAKE AN ONLINE COURSE 35

LOOK AT THE STARS 36

GET YOUR COLORS DONE 37

MAKE MUSIC PART OF EVERY DAY 38

ASK FOR HELP 39

SUPPORT ANIMALS 40

KEEP A GRATITUDE JOURNAL. 41

REFRESH YOUR THINKING WITH PEPPERMINT OIL. 42

TALK DIRTY. 43

BALANCE YOUR BRAIN'S HEMISPHERES. 44

PRESENT A BETTER IMAGE. 45

VACUUM UP MENTAL STRESS. 46

BUY FAIR TRADE PRODUCTS 47

READ A LOVE POEM 48

MAKE A MANDALA. 49

TELL THE TRUTH 50

RE-EVALUATE WHAT YOU HAVE. 51

START A WISH BOOK. 52

SPEND TIME DAYDREAMING. 53

WEAR PASTELS TO LIGHTEN UP 54

CONTEMPLATE YOUR DESIRED QUALITIES. 55

LISTEN TO THE SOOTHING SOUND OF WATER 56

INCREASE YOUR ATTENTION SPAN. 57

FIND A NEW HOBBY. 58

REVISIT A TIME OF ABUNDANCE 59

BREAK UP YOUR SCHEDULE. 60

PAY YOURSELF FIRST. 61

SAY IT WITH ROSES. 62

CONTEMPLATE A ZEN KOAN 63

PART 2: BODY 65

INDULGE YOUR TASTE BUDS 66

EASE PAIN WITH ACUPRESSURE. 67

ENJOY THE GIFTS OF GINGER. 68

TAP YOUR PSYCHIC HEALING POWER 69

SIP HIBISCUS TEA 70

WALK IN A QUIET PLACE. 71

SUPPLEMENT YOUR STAMINA. 72

ASSUME THE WARRIOR YOGA POSE. 73

DEFY SKIN AGING. 74

BALANCE YOUR CHAKRAS 75

TAKE A NEW ROUTE. 76

EXFOLIATE WITH SEA SALT 77

DRUM TO HARMONIZE YOUR HEARTBEAT. 78

EAT LOCAL PRODUCE 79

STRENGTHEN YOUR HEART. 80

CONSIDER ROLFING THERAPY 81

HEAL WOUNDS WITH CALENDULA CREAM 82

DANCE FREELY. 83

EAT A FOOD YOU DON'T THINK YOU'LL LIKE 84

USE THE BREATH OF FIRE TO GET ENERGIZED. 85

WALK IN BALANCE. 86

LISTEN TO YOUR BODY TALK 87

ENGAGE BOTH YIN AND YANG ENERGIES. 88

GO SOMEWHERE NEW. 89

SOOTHE YOUR SKIN WITH ALOE. 90

OPEN YOUR HEART WITH YOGA'S FISH POSE 91

TAKE RESCUE REMEDY. 92

USE KINESIOLOGY TO EXPLORE YOUR NEEDS 93

TRY BLACK CURRANT SEED OIL 94

STAND UP STRAIGHT. 95

DO TAI CHI 96

GET NUTTY. 97

DO NECK ROLLS AT YOUR DESK. 98

TREAT YOUR SKIN WITH CEDAR OIL 99

BREAK UP YOUR WORKOUT 100

SWITCH TO GLASS CONTAINERS 101

TREAT YOURSELF TO SCENTED SOAP 102

UP YOUR OMEGA-3S. 103

FIND EXCUSES TO EXERCISE 104

CHANGE YOUR DAILY ROUTINE 105

SING. 106

PICK UP TRASH WHEN YOU WALK 107

TRY HAND REFLEXOLOGY 108

PARK FAR AWAY. 109

EAT SEA VEGETABLES 110

OPEN YOUR WINDOWS 111

REACH OUT AND TOUCH SOMEONE 112

TRY A NEW TYPE OF WORKOUT 113

EAT TO A MORE YOUTHFUL YOU 114

DO THE TWIST 115

PART 3: SPIRIT 117

LIFT YOUR SPIRITS WITH ROSE QUARTZ. 118

PROTECT YOUR HOME WITH AN EYE AMULET. 119

ENCOURAGE SOMEONE'S SPIRITUAL GROWTH. 120

MAKE AN OFFERING 121

GET ANSWERS WITH A PENDULUM. 122

CLEANSE YOUR ENERGY FIELD WITH PERIDOT 123

INCREASE THE SWEETNESS IN YOUR LIFE. 124

TAP THE POWER OF THREE 125

SWITCH UP YOUR ARTWORK 126

USE AFFIRMATIONS TO INCREASE YOUR PROSPERITY 127

OBSERVE SIGNS FROM THE UNIVERSE 128

ENGAGE IN SPIRITUAL SHARING. 129

MEDITATE ON THE CHARIOT CARD. 130

LISTEN TO WIND CHIMES 131

CONSULT THE *I CHING*. 132

PRACTICE NONVIOLENCE. 133

PROTECT YOURSELF WITH AMBER. 134

CHOOSE A PERSONAL SYMBOL 135

CHART YOUR POWER DAYS. 136

IMPRINT WATER WITH YOUR INTENTIONS 137

DO SOMETHING CHILDISH 138

CONTACT AN ANGEL 139

SEEK HELP FROM YOUR SPIRIT ANIMAL. 140

LOOK FOR AURAS. 141

PACK A TRAVEL ALTAR. 142

WEAR YELLOW TOPAZ FOR CONFIDENCE 143

FOLLOW MERCURY 144

LIFT YOUR SPIRITS WITH GRAPEFRUIT. 145

TAP IN TO ESP 146

SEND POSITIVE ENERGY TO YOUR SKIN 147

CONTEMPLATE THE LOTUS SYMBOL 148

REMOVE COMPUTER STRESS WITH TOURMALINE. 149

HEAL OLD WOUNDS. 150

OPEN YOUR THIRD EYE 151

CONTEMPLATE THE STRENGTH CARD 152

EXPLORE THE SPACE BETWEEN BREATHS. 153

GAZE INTO YOUR LOVED ONE'S EYES. 154

SMILE INWARDLY. 155

MAKE A TALISMAN 156

CONSULT THE RUNES. 157

TAP IN TO THE ENERGY OF MARS 158

LISTEN TO YOUR BACK. 159

HEAL YOUR HEART WITH RUBY IN ZOISITE 160

USE THE LOVERS CARD TO ENHANCE INTIMACY 161

LEARN ABOUT YOUR SUN SIGN. 162

INVITE A DEITY'S BLESSING 163

EXAMINE YOUR HEART LINES. 164

SILENTLY BLESS OTHERS 165

GET DAILY E-INSPIRATION 166

ATTEND AN UNFAMILIAR RITUAL OR CEREMONY 167

Index. 169

INTRODUCTION

Do you want to learn how to beat stress
and prioritize what matters most?
Are you looking for ways to improve your health and boost energy?
Do you want to feel more in tune with yourself
and the world around you?

If you answered yes to any of these questions, you're looking for self-care!

My Pocket Self-Care offers 150 exercises you can do at home, at work, or on the go to help you care for your mind, body, and spirit. These fast but powerful exercises will help you balance every part of your mental, physical, and emotional health, in order to flourish as the best version of you possible.

You'll learn how to care for and maintain all of your needs by completing simple activities like:

* Manifesting courage through Warrior Pose
* Refreshing your thinking with peppermint oil
* Finding answers with a pendulum
* Reinvigorating your skin with vitamin C

* Creating a personal mission statement
* Removing computer stress with a tourmaline crystal

As you delve into these exercises, keep in mind that they don't follow a strict order. If you feel drawn to a certain topic, or are looking for self-care in a specific area, skip straight to it. The rest will be here waiting for you whenever you are ready. It's time to take charge of your health and happiness with self-care, so turn the page and let's get started!

PART 1
MIND

CONSIDER HOW EMOTIONS AFFECT YOUR DECISIONS

Do you often find yourself nervous, anxious, irritable, or tense? If so, you're not alone. According to a *Prevention* magazine survey, three-quarters of those polled said they experienced "great stress" one day a week.

When you are stressed out, it can be difficult to make sound decisions. If you are upset, anxious, or in a bad mood, you may sub-consciously revisit a situation from your past that hooks into your emotional state, and make a decision based on that earlier situation, rather than the facts of the current one. Realizing how your own emotions impact the choices you make can help you discern when it is best to put off a decision until you are in a calmer frame of mind.

ORGANIZE GOALS
INTO STEPS

Everything in our world began with a dream or vision. But you must bring your dreams down to earth if you want them to materialize. It's time to focus on making your dreams realities.

Break down larger goals into small steps. Not only will this give you a plan of action for where to go from here, but it will also make the dream itself feel achievable, and help you stay the course no matter what obstacles may crop up along the way.

TRACK
NEGATIVE THOUGHTS

According to the tenets of Hinduism, thoughts are as powerful as spoken words and produce reactions, either good or bad, according to what you think about. It's a good reason to be positive in your thoughts, words, and deeds.

Unfortunately, negative thoughts have a way of multiplying—fast. And if you let them, they'll drag you down into the dumps. Start monitoring your thoughts. Every time you catch yourself thinking about something unpleasant, immediately shift to something positive. It may also help to write down the negative thoughts you have, either in a journal or a note in your smartphone, so you can see just how often they creep in. Keep a few feel-good thoughts handy as well, and go to them whenever you need to dispel negativity.

CREATE A PERSONAL MISSION STATEMENT

When you look behind an "overnight success," you'll usually discover someone who has worked long and hard to get ahead. Edison may have been right when he said genius is 99 percent perspiration—in other words, effort and persistence.

Companies usually state their core values in "mission statements." A mission statement tells customers, community, workers, and others what your purpose is and what your business is all about. You can do the same thing! Create a personal mission statement that describes your vision and goals—for example, "My personal mission is to get my students excited about learning and inspire them to pursue what they are passionate about." A personal mission statement will help keep you on track when challenges crop up.

CEASE MULTITASKING

Our fast-paced society encourages us to keep doing more things faster, yet the result is often increased stress and diminished quality of life. Instead of speeding up, try slowing down and focusing on one thing at a time. You may discover you enjoy time with loved ones more, feel more relaxed, and even perform better-quality work.

In fact, according to a study published in the American Psychological Association's *Journal of Experimental Psychology*, multitasking actually reduces productivity instead of increasing it. When you do many things at once, you can't commit to doing any of them well. Make a point of giving each task your full attention. If you're talking to a friend on the phone, turn off the TV. If you're eating breakfast, don't read the newspaper at the same time.

ESTABLISH PERSONAL BOUNDARIES

One of the best ways to improve your mental health is to reduce stress. Numerous studies have demonstrated that chronic stress can lead to serious conditions including depression, anxiety, and PTSD. You may not be able to live a completely stress-free existence, but you can minimize the effects of stress by changing the way you react to outside stressors.

If you are a person who often gets dumped on or asked for help, you may need to set boundaries for yourself. Otherwise, people can take advantage of your kindness, and their demands will build up your stress. Establish rules at home and at work and enforce them. Learn to say no without feeling guilty.

REFOCUS WITH DHARANA

For thousands of years, people have practiced yoga for mental health. Through yoga, you can rejuvenate, care for, and nurture yourself at the deepest levels, which has a positive impact on your relationships with others. Most importantly, you will develop a better relationship with yourself.

Stilling the restless mind is a main goal in yoga and meditation; however, it can often feel difficult when you are first starting out (or when life is particularly chaotic). A yoga practice known as dharana makes this easier by having you focus on a single object in order to still your mind. Choose either something living or something inorganic and hold your gaze on this object as you breathe in and out. When your mind is still, you can better focus on a particular task, or determine what should be prioritized.

NOURISH
A HIDDEN TALENT

Your biggest obstacle to health and happiness is often yourself. You may not even notice some of the ways you might be limiting yourself, including those deeper feelings of inadequacy or fear of judgment from others that can bubble up when you consider pursuing something new or enjoyable. It's time to get out of your own way and let your light shine.

Have you always wanted to draw or write poetry but were afraid you weren't good enough? Unless you try, you'll never know. Many people erroneously believe they don't have talent because they expect instant success. But like anything else, you have to practice to become good. Put your expectations on hold and just experiment. Having fun is the first step.

FIND OPPORTUNITIES
IN DELAYS

Positive and negative can be viewed as two sides of the same coin. Do you usually see a problem or an opportunity in a situation? To manifest a more positive outlook on life, it's important to find ways to make the best of a challenging circumstance.

When your flight is delayed, your train doesn't arrive on time, your doctor is running behind on appointments, or your friend is late for lunch, turn a negative into a positive:

* Read a book
* Send a few emails or text messages
* Call a loved one
* Take some quiet time for yourself
* Review a guidebook or blog post of must-see places if you're traveling to a new destination

Instead of seeing this as time wasted, relish it as extra moments to do what you please.

RECONSIDER YOUR PRIORITIES

A good life isn't necessarily a long one; rather, it's one in which you embrace joy every step of the way. Joseph Campbell often recommended, "Follow your bliss." The best way to care for yourself and perhaps live a long, healthy life is to fill your days with meaning on every level.

When you look back on your life, will you be happier knowing you did the things you wanted to do or that you did the things you were supposed to do? In their later years, few people say they regretted not spending more hours at the office. Instead, they wish they'd made more time for friends, family, and hobbies or interests they prized. It's never too late to devote time to the people and things you love—all you have to do is make them a priority. Consider what your own priorities are: Make a list, if you desire, to better help you reflect on each.

IMPROVE YOUR VOCABULARY

Although science suggests we use only a small percentage of our brains, studies have shown that we have many methods available to us for improving brain power. Diet, exercise, meditation, and many other practices can improve mental function.

One simple way to keep your mind sharp and perhaps prevent age-related deterioration is to give it plenty of exercise. Consider working those mental muscles by improving your vocabulary by learning a new word every day. The English language is constantly evolving and now contains over one million words—plenty to choose from! You can even download a Word of the Day app on your smartphone.

JOIN A
SOCIAL CLUB

Science has managed to extend our lives quite impressively. Yet attitude and lifestyle, as much as technology, are responsible for not only the length of your life but its quality as well. Take steps to ensure you have the life you desire.

The more people participate in social relationships, the better their overall mental health. The MacArthur Foundation Research Network on Successful Aging revealed that the two strongest predictors of well-being among the elderly are frequency of visits with friends and frequency of attendance at organization meetings. The more diverse your circle of social support, the happier you are likely to be.

BALANCE YOUR MINDSET
WITH GINSENG

Ginseng is a valuable root that's been used for millennia in Eastern medicine to heal a wide range of ailments, including stress and mental fatigue. Note: Siberian ginseng isn't actually ginseng, though it has many of the same health benefits.

Herbalists and practitioners of Eastern medicine categorize herbs as "heating" or "cooling" and use them to heal accordingly. Asian ginseng is considered heating; American ginseng is considered cooling. When you need a mental pick-me-up, try the Asian variety. If you want to calm stress, use the American version. You can enjoy the benefits in a steaming cup of ginseng tea, cut up the root to add to soup, or consume it raw.

FOCUS ON FORGIVENESS

Psychologists have found that dwelling on past hurts can increase stress. In one study, stress diminished when subjects thought about forgiveness. Further research also links a lack of forgiveness to anxiety, depression, and strained relationships. Forgiving others is key in being your happiest, healthiest self.

Think about someone you are feeling hurt by or disappointed in. You can write a letter to this person, even if you decide not to send it, or visualize a conversation with them. Tell them you forgive them, and that it's in the past. Notice how you feel as you put down the burden of anger, pain, or resentment you've been carrying.

MIST YOUR CAR
WITH LAVENDER

One of the most dangerous things you can do is drive a car. In the United States alone, more than forty thousand people die on the roadways each year. That's why it's a great idea for everyone to set the intention to be a safe and courteous driver.

Of course, driving can be extremely stressful, especially in urban areas with tons of traffic and distracting noise. Aromatherapy can help you stay calm while driving, avoiding things like road rage, which can affect how safely you drive and how you interact with other drivers. Put water in a spray bottle and add a few drops of lavender essential oil. Shake the bottle and mist the inside of your car with the fragrant blend. If you like, add some lemon or mint essential oil to also keep you more alert behind the wheel.

DETOX
WITH MUDRAS

Westerners have come to appreciate the ancient healing traditions of the East. Acupuncture, yoga, Ayurvedic medicine, meditation, and feng shui are only a few of the jewels to be gleaned from Asian cultures.

A mudra, or special hand gesture, is another gem that can give your mental health a boost. Simply curl the ring and middle fingers of each hand to touch the tip of the thumb of the same hand. Hold this posture for fifteen minutes, three times per day. Use this mudra to help you eliminate toxicity and make space for new beginnings, new ideas, and new projects.

REVEAL
YOUR FEELINGS

Many of us, having been hurt in love before, put up barriers to love. It's time to open yourself to the healing power of love.

Often, we don't express our feelings because we fear our loved ones may not respond in the way we'd like. Today, take a step toward your happiest self by revealing one thing you've been holding inside. It may be something you admire about that person, something they have done that hurt you, or something you'd like them to do.

WRITE
A HAIKU

Express your creativity. Research published in *The Washington Post* found that those who engaged in creative pursuits had increased neural activity and less depression; creativity may even lower the risk of Alzheimer's in older adults. But don't wait until you're old to get creative!

Haiku, a Japanese poetic form, traditionally uses three lines of text: the first line with five syllables, the second with seven syllables, and the third with five syllables. Many haiku poems depict subjects from nature. Try your hand at writing one. The exercise not only taps your creativity and flexes your mental muscles; it gives you an opportunity to find beauty in the world around you. See the *Encyclopaedia Britannica* at www.britannica.com/art/haiku for more information.

SHIFT YOUR ATTENTION
AWAY FROM YOURSELF

Life is a series of hills and valleys. If things aren't looking bright right now, that is sure to change. During times of adversity, it's especially important to take care of your mental health. A clear, calm mind will pave the way for new opportunities.

Take the magnifying glass off what is wrong in your life and turn your attention to other people. Who is important in your life and how are they doing today? Is there something you can do for them? When you direct your attention away from your troubles and focus on enriching the lives of others, you boost your own happiness.

HIDE A LOVE NOTE FOR SOMEONE SPECIAL

Today, let your love shine brightly. Delight in it. Proclaim it proudly. Indulge its demands and cravings. Let it bring out your best self.

Write a love note and leave it for your partner to find. Pin it to their pillow, slip it in their work bag, post it on the bathroom mirror, or tape it to their car dashboard. It can be something as simple and heartfelt as "I love you." Or copy a favorite love poem that expresses your sentiments. If you prefer, write something racy—tell your lover what you'd like to do with them later.

PICK YOUR BATTLES

You cannot control what others think, say, feel, or do. You can only control yourself and your responses to situations; others are responsible for their own actions. Accepting this can remove a great deal of stress from your life.

Determine which battles are worth fighting and which are a waste of time and energy. Choose to participate only in those you believe are worthwhile and that you have a chance of effecting positive outcomes. If a discussion starts escalating out of control, walk away and perhaps try at another time.

TAKE AN
ONLINE COURSE

Your brain, like your body, must be exercised regularly and fed properly to keep it functioning optimally. Take one step today to nourish your brain by enrolling in an online course.

Whether you want to get a college degree or just try out a class for the sheer pleasure of learning, you'll find lots of opportunities online. Brush up your skills or get certified in a special area. Some schools even allow you to design your own curriculum! For more on-the-go learning, there are free apps you can download on your smartphone: Try Khan Academy and Udemy.

LOOK AT
THE STARS

Six thousand years ago, stargazers began identifying constellations and assigning meanings to them. The ancients believed the planets and stars were the homes of gods and goddesses, who guided earthly affairs. Stars have long been symbols of hope. Today, let them guide and inspire you too.

Sit back and gaze up at the stars—just as people have done for millennia. Enjoy the tranquil beauty of the sky overhead. Flex your mental muscles by hunting for specific constellations and reflect on those who have gleaned wisdom from the stars and changed the way the world thinks about space and our own planet—Galileo Galilei, Carl Sagan, Stephen Hawking, and more.

GET YOUR
COLORS DONE

Today, notice the role color plays in your life. Even our language equates color with feelings. Are you in the pink? Feeling blue? Red hot? Color can also be used to promote emotional well-being—beginning with a simple boost in self-confidence.

Carole Jackson's book *Color Me Beautiful* examines which colors look best on you, and has popularized an entire beauty trend. It suggests that wearing certain colors enhances your hair, skin, and eyes. The method lets you choose clothing that flatters your natural coloring and complements your features, so you can look and ultimately feel your best. Once you determine your best palette, you can streamline your entire wardrobe.

MAKE MUSIC PART
OF EVERY DAY

Music influences us on many levels, soothing, enlivening, and inspiring us. A 2009 study at the Cleveland Clinic found music eased patient anxiety during surgery. Let music make your day better.

Listen to music while doing household chores, exercising, driving, shopping, or working. Classical music, in particular, eases stress, such as when you're waiting in the dentist's office or preparing for a work presentation. Use your phone or other portable device with earphones to shut out the stressors in your environment.

ASK
FOR HELP

You can't nurture others optimally unless you are nourished yourself. Unfortunately, those who regularly give to others are often the last to give to themselves.

There comes a time when you simply can't do it all yourself—and you don't have to. Friends, relatives, and neighbors are usually glad to help out in a pinch. You can return the favor at a later date. If necessary, hire the help you need: home healthcare services, lawn maintenance, housecleaning, or whatever. Set priorities, and let others handle the rest.

SUPPORT
ANIMALS

Animals can contribute so much to your happiness, well-being, and quality of life. An earthquake in Kobe, Japan, in 1995 put this notion into perspective. Dr. Gen Kato, president of the Japanese Animal Hospital Association, observed that people who had pets coped better with the crisis.

As human beings continue to encroach on animals' territory, it's up to us to provide for their welfare. Donate your money, time, or both to organizations that protect wildlife, domestic and farm animals, and creatures of all kinds. Treat all animals you encounter with kindness and respect.

KEEP A
GRATITUDE JOURNAL

Feeling down? In a creative rut? It's time to open your mind to the opportunities and blessings the universe has to offer you!

One of the steps to manifesting what you desire is being grateful. Every day, write down something you are thankful for. Expressing thanks for the good things you already have lifts your mind to a more positive place. A negative mindset sabotages possibilities before you even get started; with a positive mindset, you are more likely to attract positive things, people, and situations.

REFRESH YOUR THINKING
WITH PEPPERMINT OIL

Since ancient times, herbs have been used for healing. According to a survey by the National Center for Health Statistics (part of the Centers for Disease Control and Prevention), more than half of Americans use complementary and alternative therapies, including herbal medicine. One of the most versatile (and tastiest!) herbs is peppermint.

The fresh, clean scent of peppermint can stimulate your mind when your attention starts to fade. If you've been plodding along at a boring or mentally taxing task, put a few drops of peppermint essential oil on a cloth handkerchief and smell it. You can also use a diffuser to release the scent throughout any room. Peppermint instantly reaches your brain and boosts your alertness.

TALK
DIRTY

Make a commitment to enjoy your sex life more. As repeated studies have shown, intimacy is good for your mental health. People in loving relationships report having more fulfilling sex, and fulfilling sex helps keep that bond strong: It's a cycle worth nurturing.

The mind has been called the most sensitive erogenous zone. Entice it with sexy sayings. Become the narrator in your own X-rated movie. Tell your lover what you find desirable about them. Explain what you want to do with your partner and how it makes you feel. Be explicit and get down to the nitty-gritty.

BALANCE YOUR BRAIN'S HEMISPHERES

Your brain is your most important organ, the body's control tower. Its more than 100 billion cells send commands to direct all your other cells. In most people, the brain declines with age; however, you can take steps to slow this process.

Use this breathing exercise to encourage the two sides of your brain to work together harmoniously:

1. Hold your left nostril shut and inhale through your right nostril.
2. Hold for a count of ten, then exhale through your mouth.
3. Repeat three times.
4. Switch sides and repeat three times.

Once you get the hang of it, you can do this exercise anytime, anywhere.

PRESENT A
BETTER IMAGE

You are as powerful as you believe yourself to be. Most of us underestimate ourselves and resign ourselves to being less than we could be. Today, take steps to boost your self-confidence. When you believe in yourself, other people will too.

Hone your public speaking skills by signing up for an online class, downloading an app on your smartphone like Orai or Toastmasters International, or following *YouTube* tutorials. You'll discover dozens of tips and can even get feedback to help you present yourself more effectively, whether you're interviewing for a job or giving a wedding toast.

VACUUM UP
MENTAL STRESS

Cleanliness has long been linked with wellness. The word *hygiene* derives from Hygieia, who was the Greek goddess of health. And tidying up doesn't just happen on the outside: Through a little inner cleaning, you can improve your mental health without lifting a finger.

Sit in a quiet place and close your eyes. Take several slow, deep breaths to relax. When you feel ready, imagine the stress and problems in your life as dirt on a carpet. Then envision yourself using a vacuum cleaner to suck up all the dirt that has been distressing you. Continue vacuuming up annoyances until your mental environment is clean and you feel relaxed.

BUY FAIR TRADE PRODUCTS

When it comes to saving the planet, every little bit helps. It's increasingly obvious that we are dependent on one another and our environment, and doing your part to live more lightly on the earth encourages not just your own health and happiness, but also the health and happiness of all beings. Just one small act will boost your mood, make you feel more connected to other people, and help someone in need.

When you buy fair trade products, you show support for a more equitable distribution of business risks and rewards between owners and workers in a global economy. The Fair Trade Federation seeks to eliminate forced child labor and to establish fair compensation for labor, workplace safety, and freedom from discrimination. Look for the "fair trade" label on products you purchase.

READ A
LOVE POEM

A study at the State University of New York found that the brains of people in love were rich in dopamine, a feel-good chemical that reduces stress, increases motivation, aids in memory, and helps keep you focused. Love, it appears, not only makes the world go 'round; it makes us healthier as well!

Enjoy reading a poem that inspires loving feelings in you. If possible, share the poem with someone you care about. It may be a romantic poem or one that speaks to a more all-compassionate love, such as the spiritual works of the Sufi poets Hafiz and Rumi. Allow tender, loving feelings to arise in you.

MAKE A MANDALA

Life is a balancing act. And if you are struggling to keep too many balls in the air, it's time to focus on finding harmony. Today, take a simple step to establish equilibrium from within.

Mandala means "circle" in Sanskrit. These elaborate, circular paintings symbolically depict the universe, with the heavens at the top and earth at the bottom. They also represent your own inner and outer nature, thus signifying unity and harmony. Draw your own mandala to bring your mind into balance. Include symbols, images, and colors that are meaningful for you.

TELL
THE TRUTH

Set an intention to be totally honest today. If someone asks you something you don't want to answer, don't resort to a little white lie to save face. Say: "Why do you want to know?" or "I'd rather not respond to that now."

Honesty develops trust between people and leads to meaningful, responsible relationships. Although telling the truth can be difficult at times, doing so removes the burden of guilt and the potential need to concoct more lies to cover up previous ones. Speaking your own truth also lets you value yourself, rather than compromising yourself to suit someone else's expectations.

RE-EVALUATE
WHAT YOU HAVE

What's important to you, and why? Are your material possessions serving these priorities? Or are they cluttering your space and thoughts, keeping you from focusing on what does matter?

In our consumer-oriented society, we often spend so much time in the pursuit of wealth and possessions that we forget to ask whether we actually need what we are buying. We may also start to lose track of the items that do bring us real joy, as the stuff piles up and we focus on that next, trendy thing. Spend some time reflecting on what you own and how each item fits into what is important to you. Consider donating anything that doesn't fit this picture.

START A
WISH BOOK

Pursue opportunities that seem right to you, even if other people think you're nuts. What if J.K. Rowling had not followed her inspiration to write about the adolescent wizard Harry Potter? Or if Ralph Lauren had been afraid to use his tie designs to found his own company? Let your heart be your guide.

Writing down what you seek in life brings your dreams one step closer to reality. Create a wish book, in which you write what you intend to materialize in terms of career, relationships, health, and so on. Read through your wish book whenever possible and update it regularly.

SPEND TIME DAYDREAMING

Whether your dreams are of the waking or sleeping variety, they stir your imagination. Imagination precedes manifestation. Everything you see in the world, from your smartphone to your car, started in someone's imagination.

The Law of Attraction tells us that daydreaming is an important step to creating the reality we desire. Before you can bring something into your life, you must first be able to imagine it. Spend time imagining the things, people, and situations you wish to draw to you. The richer and more vivid your daydreams, the more magnetic power they have.

WEAR PASTELS
TO LIGHTEN UP

When you're stressed or feeling negative, it affects every part of your day. Tasks take longer to complete, as you are likely to get caught up in overwhelmed and anxious emotions, and your relationships with others may be strained. You can be happier and healthier, too, when you lighten up and approach your day in a more relaxed manner.

Psychological researchers have found that colors have the ability to influence emotional and physical reactions. To lighten your mood, wear pastels. Yellow can help you feel more optimistic; light blue gives a sense of peace and calm; pink makes you feel more friendly and affectionate.

CONTEMPLATE YOUR
DESIRED QUALITIES

Intimacy keeps you happy. It helps you manage stress, and keeps you connected to the person you love. Take the first step in making your love life a fulfilling one.

Imagine your ideal partner. List the qualities you find most attractive. Kindness? Self-confidence? Fidelity? Your A list should include the most crucial qualities; your B list can include other important characteristics that aren't deal-breakers. The clearer you are, the better your chances of attracting that person. And if you currently have a partner, your list of crucial qualities is something you will want to consider in the relationship. You may also want to start a dialogue with the other person to communicate these desires and check in on what items may be in need of more attention.

LISTEN TO THE SOOTHING SOUND OF WATER

More than 70 percent of the earth is covered by water. Up to 60 percent of your body is water. Water is everywhere, and its healing effects extend far beyond simple hydration.

Listening to the soothing sounds of water can calm stress, promote mental relaxation, and help you sleep better. Even if you don't live near an ocean, lake, or river, you can still enjoy the peaceful sounds of moving water. Install a fountain or water garden inside or outside your home. Or download an app on your smartphone that features the sounds of rippling brooks and waves breaking on the shore. Some bedside clocks even offer different water sounds to lull you to sleep.

INCREASE YOUR ATTENTION SPAN

It's estimated that the maximum attention span for adults is about twenty minutes, and just three to five minutes for children. Increasing your ability to focus on a task can help you become more successful, as you are less likely to fall prey to the countless distractions of everyday life.

To boost your attention span, spend some time reading a book or magazine. *Publishers Weekly*, the principal trade magazine for the book business, says the average person spends just 2.1 hours a month reading: That's less than 1 percent of the entire month! On top of an increased attention span, reading more often can improve your creative ability by stimulating the formation of mental images as you read words. It also boosts your vocabulary and can help you retain cognitive abilities later in life.

FIND A
NEW HOBBY

Everyone wants to enjoy a healthy life. Even if you have cultivated great mental health in one moment, you still have to do the regular maintenance. You wouldn't expect your car to keep performing well if you didn't take care of it. The same is true of your mind.

According to Daniel G. Amen, MD, in *Making a Good Brain Great*, it's better to learn something new than to repeat the same activities: "When the brain does something over and over, even a complicated task, it learns how to do it using less and less energy." Try a hobby that requires coordination between multiple brain regions, such as knitting, gardening, or writing poetry.

REVISIT A
TIME OF ABUNDANCE

Abundance is more than money and possessions—it's a state of feeling comfortable and content with your life on every level, knowing that you have everything you need. In their bestselling books, Esther and Jerry Hicks recommend imagining yourself enjoying all the things money can buy in order to attract prosperity.

A good way to engage your imagination is to step back into the past. Think about a time when you received something you desired; use as many of your senses as you can to paint a vivid picture. What did that abundance look like? Were there any sounds or tactile sensations tied to it? How did your own body feel in that moment? Once you have been fully immersed in that memory, you can shift your focus to envisioning good things coming to you now.

BREAK UP
YOUR SCHEDULE

If you're like many people, you may find yourself burning the candle at both ends from time to time. There never seem to be enough hours in the day to accomplish everything. Now could be the time to reverse that trend.

You can actually be more productive if you break up the pace of your day. Instead of working for hours and hours on one task, which can lead to burnout, design a pattern that fits your needs. For instance, work at your desk for an hour, then get up and do something else for ten minutes—go to the copy machine, take a quick walk, do the laundry, or eat a healthy snack. Balance intense mental focus with relaxation and creative time to keep your energy up and your mind sharp for longer.

PAY YOURSELF
FIRST

Are you feeling the pinch of economic woes? Perhaps it's time to look at more than just the recommendations of financial gurus. You may want to consider other factors that affect your fiscal well-being—and ultimately your happiness.

Before you pay your bills, pay yourself: Deposit a set amount of money from each paycheck into a savings account. This form of savings lets you acknowledge your worthiness and helps you value yourself more. As your nest egg grows, you'll also feel proud of yourself for managing to put away money on a steady basis.

SAY IT
WITH ROSES

No flower is more beloved and symbolic than the rose. Poets, artists, gardeners, and of course lovers have long drawn inspiration from the rose—you can too.

We often associate all roses with love and romance. But in the Victorian period, the different colors of roses were assigned specific meanings, and sending a bouquet was a way to send any message of your choosing. Red roses signify passion; pink ones represent happiness. White roses mean innocence, but also "I am worthy of you." Yellow ones can indicate friendship. Send someone roses to convey your intentions and make their day *and* yours.

CONTEMPLATE
A ZEN KOAN

You only have one brain. Take care of it. Like your body, your mind needs to be exercised to continue working properly. Fortunately, there are simple activities you can do anytime to help keep your brain healthy.

A koan is a story, question, puzzle, or thought-provoking idea that cannot be analyzed with the logical mind. One well-known koan asks: "What is the sound of one hand clapping?" Zen practitioners use koans to gain insight through intuition. Try contemplating a koan yourself to exercise your mental powers. You can find dozens of Zen koan puzzles online; pick one to work through while waiting at the doctor's office, during your morning train ride to work, or as a weekend activity with your partner.

PART 2
BODY

INDULGE YOUR
TASTE BUDS

Are you selling yourself short? Self-care involves valuing yourself and treating yourself with respect. Self-deprecation can lead to depression, anxiety, and physical illness. Today, stop beating yourself up and do something nice for yourself instead.

Eat something truly extravagant and delicious, something you might ordinarily forgo because you think it's too expensive, such as caviar, Kobe beef steak, handmade dark chocolates, or champagne. Consume it slowly and savor every bit. As you enjoy your treat, tell yourself you're worth it.

EASE PAIN
WITH ACUPRESSURE

On-the-job stress and long hours at the computer can bring on a tension headache, back pain, and more. Fortunately, acupressure can offer easy, free relief whenever you are in need.

To ease the pain of a headache, close your eyes and press your index and middle fingers to the spot between your eyebrows, where your nose meets your forehead. This is known as the third eye point. Hold for at least a minute. Release, and press again. Repeat as necessary. To reduce aches, weakness, and stiffness in the lumbar area, apply light, steady pressure to the acupressure points known as Sea of Vitality for a few minutes. These points are located waist high, about two finger-widths out on either side of your spine. And if you're suffering from motion sickness while on the go, put two fingertips on the acupressure point P5, about three finger-widths up from your wrist on the underside of your arm. Hold until queasiness subsides. Acupressure can even be used to stimulate memory. When you want to recall something, activate what are known in acupressure as the Sun Points, located on your temples. Press your fingers gently, but firmly, to these points and hold for about a minute to ease mental stress, clear your head, and improve your memory.

ENJOY THE
GIFTS OF GINGER

The spicy Asian herb ginger has been used for thousands of years, both for culinary and medicinal purposes. One of the most versatile healers, it aids respiratory, digestive, muscular, and circulatory complaints. Add zing to your meals and to your health with ginger.

Ginger is particularly beneficial to digestion. Its cleansing properties help ease indigestion and stomach upsets, as well as diarrhea. Spicy ginger is also stimulating, so it can be useful for people who have lost their appetite. Grind it fresh for salads and stir-fry dishes, or drink refreshing ginger tea.

TAP YOUR PSYCHIC HEALING POWER

Each step in humankind's progress required believing in something the majority of people dismissed. Two hundred years ago, for instance, few people would have believed men would walk on the moon. Your beliefs surrounding what is and isn't possible shape how you think about the world and yourself. They can elevate your abilities or hold them back. It's time to push the boundaries of what you believe and harness your inner healing power.

The next time you injure yourself slightly—a small cut, burn, or bruise—tap your psychic power to heal yourself. Use your attention to direct soothing green light to the injured site. Then instead of focusing on the injury, envision yourself completely healed. Repeat several times a day, for a minute or so at a time. You may just find you heal more quickly than you normally would.

SIP
HIBISCUS TEA

For centuries, people have enjoyed tea for its vast health purposes. A 2010 Alzheimer's Association study found that seniors who drank tea experienced better cognitive function than those who didn't. Caffeine-free tea is also a great source of hydration when you feel bored with plain water.

Hibiscus is a tropical flower favored for both its floral taste and wonderful health benefits. It is packed with antioxidants that help prevent cell damage and disease caused by free radicals. Hibiscus can also lower blood pressure, boost liver function, and promote weight loss. Enjoy hibiscus tea whether at home or on the go.

WALK IN A
QUIET PLACE

Withdraw from the noise and activity that characterize your everyday life and devote a little time to quiet contemplation. Mahatma Gandhi was silent one day each week because he felt it helped him find inner peace. Because your body rhythms, breathing, and stress levels slow when you stop speaking, silence can also offer health benefits.

Find a quiet place where you can walk alone, without talking to anyone. It can be a path near your home, or an alternative route to a local shop. Try not to let your thoughts run to everyday matters. Allow your senses to appreciate things you might not notice ordinarily—smells; the ground beneath your feet; the wind, sun, or rain on your face; etc. Studies show that taking short, quiet walks regularly can lower your risk for diabetes and heart disease. Fresh air and gentle exercise do any body good.

SUPPLEMENT YOUR STAMINA

Self-care means not pushing yourself so hard that you get stressed out or even sick. In 2010, the BBC reported that working overtime regularly increases your risk of heart attack. Type A people also get sick more and may be more likely to suffer from anxiety and depression. Be persistent, but don't push yourself to the breaking point.

DHEA, a hormone naturally supplied by the adrenal glands, can be diminished by disease, stress, aging, and other factors. When DHEA levels are low, you may become depressed, discouraged, tired, or ill. Some studies show that supplementing with DHEA can aid adrenal fatigue, which may give you more energy to do what you need to do. To give your body a boost, look for a DHEA supplement online or in any health food store.

ASSUME THE WARRIOR YOGA POSE

You may have heard the phrase "your body is a temple," and it's true. Complete wellness includes nourishing the vessel that moves you from one day to the next. And a healthy, capable body often sets the stage for how you feel internally as well. When you feel physically strong, you feel mentally strong too. The daily challenges at work and home are less daunting and setbacks can be taken in stride.

One simple way to build strength is through Warrior Pose. To assume this yoga position, first stand with your legs as far apart as is comfortable, with your right leg in front and your left leg behind. Bend your right leg at the knee and keep your left leg straight. Hold your arms straight, parallel to the ground, with your right arm stretched out in front, above your right knee, and your left arm behind you. Maintain the posture for a minute or two, then change legs. As you hold the pose, reflect on how powerful this open, stable position is already making you feel.

DEFY
SKIN AGING

It's often said that youth isn't just a physical condition, but a state of mind. When you feel vibrant, that energy radiates in every part of your being, from your outward appearance to your inner confidence. Today, invest in a little self-care that combats aging where it often shows the most: your skin.

Vitamin C is an important part of the release and regulation of collagen in your skin. Collagen is what keeps skin elastic and repairs damage such as sunburn. Studies have found that a diet high in vitamin C is linked to better skin appearance and fewer wrinkles, while a topical vitamin C cream can diminish wrinkles and reduce skin roughness over time.

BALANCE
YOUR CHAKRAS

Images have a real impact on your body, according to David Sobel, MD, and Robert Ornstein, PhD, the authors of *Mind & Body Health Handbook*. You can use imagination to reduce pain, as well as calm stress and eliminate bad habits. The more you practice, the better you'll get.

When the body's seven main energy centers, known as the chakras, are blocked or out of balance, illness can occur. To eliminate energy blockages and get your chakras back into balance, close your eyes and imagine red light glowing at your root chakra (at the base of the spine), orange at your sacral chakra (in your lower belly), yellow at your solar plexus chakra (just below the rib cage), green at your heart chakra (in the center of the chest), blue at your throat chakra, indigo at your third eye chakra (between your eyebrows), and violet at your crown chakra (at the top of your head). Do this exercise daily to keep your energy centers functioning optimally.

TAKE A
NEW ROUTE

We tend to get locked into patterns that can block opportunities for new experiences and slowly drain our motivation to continue activities that are good for our health. Change is the nature of life, the only thing we can be sure of. Nothing remains the same forever. Embrace it today.

Walk (or bike if you prefer!) to a place you go frequently—but this time, take a different route than usual. Observe how the terrain looks when seen from a new direction. Notice how it feels to cover familiar territory in an unfamiliar way. Pay attention to your body's signals—how do you react when you shift your predictable regimen? Do you find it stimulating? Refreshing?

EXFOLIATE
WITH SEA SALT

Although many Americans tend to go overboard, salt is essential for good health—at least 500 milligrams per day, according to the National Academy of Sciences. This essential mineral has a colorful history too; it influenced the development of cities and played a role in wars.

Salt is also a great addition to your skincare routine. Regular exfoliation with salt produces healthier-looking skin and aids the development of new collagen. Make an exfoliating scrub using sea salt by combining one part oil (such as sweet almond) and two parts sea salt to form a somewhat thick mixture. Rub liberally into your skin, then rinse.

DRUM TO HARMONIZE YOUR HEARTBEAT

We live in a world of resonance. Everything pulses with its own unique vibration. When your resonance is high, you experience well-being. When your resonance declines, so does your health. There are some things you can do to keep your body vibrating at a healthy rate.

In some Native American and African traditions, drumming is used as a way to balance and heal the heart. And you don't need a professional drum to practice this activity: Using the palms of your hands, drum a beat on your thighs that is in sync with your heart's rhythm. If your heart rate is rapid, you can calm it by playing a rhythm that is slightly slower. If you are looking to give yourself a little boost of energy, you can raise your heart rate by playing a rhythm that is slightly faster. Your heart will align itself to the drum's vibration.

EAT LOCAL PRODUCE

One of the most important factors in physical health is what goes into your body. Yet, it can be so easy to reach for fast, unhealthy options when on the go. But there are plenty of portable options you can pack for the day ahead!

Check out locally grown fruits and vegetables to enjoy as snacks or a side to your lunch. Locally grown fruits and vegetables are likely to be fresher, less processed, and more nutritious than those shipped in from other countries. According to some sources, foods that are native to your area are healthier for you because your body is in harmony with them. Additionally, imported foods may come from countries that have lower standards for chemical fertilizers and pesticides. Your body—and community—will thank you.

STRENGTHEN
YOUR HEART

What role does fear play in your life? Some fears are natural and serve a self-protective purpose. Others can hold you back from new opportunities; you may hesitate in a risk that ultimately increases your self-confidence, resilience, creativity, and competence.

The heart has long been linked with courage. We tell someone whose faith and fervor are waning to "take heart," and describe people who give it their all as "having heart." Your physical heart is also the locus of vitality, and one way to keep it strong is by consuming hawthorn. The herb has been scientifically proven to lower high blood pressure, ease angina, regulate arrhythmia, and improve circulation. You can take it as an extract, or in a tea.

CONSIDER ROLFING THERAPY

Myths and fairy tales often illustrate the search for union and acceptance of the rejected part that resides within us. As Wilhelm Reich, Carl Jung, and other noted psychoanalysts have explained, denying things we don't like about ourselves can cause physical (as well as mental and social) dysfunction. Bringing them into consciousness awakens power and promotes overall health.

Rolfing is a form of bodywork that involves deep muscle massage and connective tissue massage to provide structural integration. Developed by Dr. Ida Rolf, this technique works to harmonize the entire body. In the process, deeply held emotions that have become trapped in the body's musculature may be released. In their place you can find more comfort with both your body and your inner sense of self. Find out more about Rolfing online and decide whether it is a good fit for you.

HEAL WOUNDS WITH CALENDULA CREAM

Enjoy the gifts of sunny yellow and orange marigolds today. These hardy and cheerful annual plants can survive in many climates and are a sure sign of summer. They also have long-standing medicinal properties. Some are even edible and add a spicy or tangy touch to salads and vegetable dishes (make sure they are safe before you ingest them).

Calendula is a type of marigold with numerous healing properties. This gentle remedy soothes cuts, scrapes, burns, cracked and chapped skin, eczema, and other minor skin problems. You can find calendula in cream or salve form in health food stores or online. Apply it directly to your skin, according to directions, to bring healing relief.

DANCE
FREELY

Many of the limits in our lives are self-imposed. Today, prepare to relax those limitations and experience the freedom that comes as a result. It's time to loosen your fetters and express your true self.

You don't have to follow carefully prescribed dance steps to get the health benefits of dancing. Trance dance, ecstatic dance, and spiritual dance are terms used for free-form dancing, which enables people to dance their own way, with or without a partner. These expressive movements are centered in ancient cultural traditions. Beyond a fun workout, you'll get those creative juices flowing, and gain a boost of energy to keep you motivated in your pursuits. You'll find free-form dance groups in most major cities, and perhaps in your own community.

EAT A FOOD
YOU DON'T THINK YOU'LL LIKE

Are you in a dinner rut? Have you fallen into the same meal plan week after week? Expand your horizons today and breathe new life into your nutrition.

Often, we refuse to try a particular food because it sounds or looks strange. We simply assume we won't like it, but that may not be the case. Today, select a food you've never eaten before but think you won't like—octopus, sushi, or beef tongue, for example. You might be pleasantly surprised! For even more health benefits, you can check out superfoods like kale, sardines, or prunes that you may have passed on before.

USE THE BREATH OF FIRE
TO GET ENERGIZED

We associate fire with vitality, enthusiasm, and passion. Metaphysically, fire is one of the four elements that compose our universe (along with earth, air, and water). Practice connecting with the energy of fire today.

A breathing technique from the kundalini school of yoga called the Breath of Fire quickly revs up your energy when you're feeling sluggish. To do this technique, sit, stand, or assume another yoga posture. Inhale and exhale through your nose, using short, fast snort-like breaths. As you inhale, relax your stomach muscles. As you exhale, pull your stomach in quickly. Continue for thirty seconds or more for a surefire energy boost.

WALK
IN BALANCE

Balance is a key part of self-care for good reason. When the different aspects of your life are out of balance, your health and happiness suffer. Some important things are nourished, while others are neglected. It's time to find harmony.

Pay attention to each step as you walk, whether you're in a store, on a nature trail, or out on the town. As your left foot meets the ground, focus on what you are receiving in life. As your right foot meets the ground, consider what you can give to others. Giving and receiving are two parts of a whole, and both are necessary to achieve balance. Feel this balance being restored as you walk and reflect.

LISTEN TO
YOUR BODY TALK

We can learn a great deal from a place of detachment. When you observe yourself and others objectively—like a scientist observes an experiment—you notice things that would likely have been overlooked had you stayed within your own perspective.

Your body reacts to your thoughts and emotions. Is someone giving you a "pain in the neck"? Is something "eating at you"? These physical reactions can be clues to what's going on at a deeper level. If you ignore them, they may eventually lead to health problems. Even more surface-level issues can go unnoticed when we are rushing about our day, focused on getting things done. Try to check in with your body regularly. Start by tuning in to your feet, and then work your way up to your head.

ENGAGE BOTH
YIN AND YANG ENERGIES

Nearly 2,500 years ago, Hippocrates, considered the father of medicine, emphasized a need for body-mind balance and encouraged his patients to employ exercise, diet, and other practices to keep their bodies in balance. The ancient system of Chinese medicine also stresses the importance of balance in health—more specifically the harmonization of yin (feminine, passive, dark) and yang (masculine, active, light) energies.

To sense yin energy, sit quietly and breathe slowly, deeply. Notice that you feel calm and relaxed. To sense yang energy, move about quickly until you start to feel your breathing speed up. Notice that you feel more active and assertive.

GO
SOMEWHERE NEW

Make a point of mixing things up today. Set aside the ego's arguments—"Yes, but" and "What if"—and just take a chance. If you insist on knowing for certain how a matter will turn out before you attempt it, you will destroy the joy of discovery.

The wonder of traveling is experiencing things you could never have experienced at home: unfamiliar people, food, scenery, language, culture, etc. You may not be able to fly off to a foreign country right this minute, but you can go someplace in your own community where you've never been before. Become an explorer in your own town or city.

SOOTHE YOUR SKIN WITH ALOE

Our skin is the largest organ in our body and a crucial part of our health. Despite this, it is often one of the first things we neglect in the hustle of everyday life. Each year, it comes in contact with countless people, objects, germs, environments, and more; these challenges, combined with insufficient care, can lead to dryness and flaking, cuts and burns, and worse.

The soothing juice of the aloe vera plant, a type of succulent that grows in hot, dry climates, makes a wonderful tonic for healing and nourishing your skin. Slather the gel on sunburn to take the heat out. Rub it on minor burns to relieve pain and reduce the chance of blistering. Apply to dry patches of skin to moisturize year-round. For bonus healing, you can also drink aloe juice to calm an acid stomach or to help cool the burning sensation of an ulcer.

OPEN YOUR HEART WITH YOGA'S FISH POSE

Heart disease is the leading cause of death for both men and women, causing more than a quarter of the deaths in the United States each year, according to the Centers for Disease Control and Prevention. Is there a link between coronary disease and feelings of lovelessness? Holistic healers say yes.

Prepare for Fish Pose by lying on your back with your legs out straight. Slide your hands under your buttocks. Tighten your abdominal muscles and raise your chest, supporting yourself on your forearms and buttocks. Arch your spine and chest; press the back of your head to the floor. Feel your heart chakra and chest opening as you take several breaths. Lower your torso again to the floor and relax. Along with balancing your heart chakra, Fish Pose boosts oxygen and promotes better blood flow for a healthy, loving heart.

TAKE RESCUE REMEDY

In response to stress, everyone experiences anxiety at times. Anxiety can cause heart palpitations, sleeplessness, dizziness, headaches, and many other conditions. Many turn to drugs to ease the symptoms of mild, temporary anxiety, but these can have other effects on your health, such as fatigue and stomach upset.

In the 1930s, Dr. Edward Bach developed a series of flower essences that work to heal the body gently and naturally. The best known is Rescue Remedy—a blend of five different flowers—which calms anxiety and reduces its effects on your physical health. Put a few drops in water or under your tongue for quick relief.

USE KINESIOLOGY TO EXPLORE YOUR NEEDS

What is beneficial to one person can be neutral or even harmful to another. Our bodies have different needs based on genetics, dietary restrictions, and more. So, what does yours need? What might be more harmful than helpful to your health?

Kinesiology (a study of movement focused on biochemical, physiological, and psychological principles) lets you see which foods, medications, and supplements benefit or harm you. To try kinesiology, hold a substance in one hand and raise your other arm. Try to hold your arm up while another person tries to push it down. If the substance you're holding is bad for you, your strength/vitality will be impaired and the other person will easily be able to push your arm down. If the substance is good for you, you'll be able to resist pressure.

TRY BLACK CURRANT SEED OIL

You're only as old as you let yourself be. Today, turn back the clock and revitalize your body with a little internal self-care.

Black currant seed oil contains an anti-inflammatory agent known as gamma-linolenic acid, which can help strengthen your body's immune system. It is rich in essential fatty acids necessary for providing energy, protecting tissue, and regulating metabolism. It can also aid menstrual cramping and mood swings. Try it to maintain your vitality and feel your best. You can find it in capsule form in most health food stores and online.

STAND UP
STRAIGHT

Your self-image is both a magnet and a shield. It attracts people who can assist you and protects you from those who might wish you ill. Even if you have to "fake it 'til you make it," each small victory will strengthen your self-confidence and personal power.

You may not be able to change some things about your body in a split second, but one thing you *can* do right now to improve your image—and your health—is to stand up straight. Hold your head high, your shoulders back, your tummy tucked in, and you'll instantly feel more confident and capable. Other people will see you that way too. Good posture also enables you to breathe more deeply and eases neck and shoulder tension.

DO
TAI CHI

In Eastern philosophy, chi or qi (pronounced chee) is the life force that flows through everything—the earth, the cosmos, our bodies, and our environments. Chinese medicine, feng shui, martial arts, and other practices seek to harmonize the movement of chi through your body, your home, and your life. By balancing your personal chi, you can enjoy a happier, healthier existence.

Tai chi is an ancient martial art that combines breathing with flowing movements. According to the Mayo Clinic, tai chi (pronounced tie-chee) may aid balance, flexibility, sleep dysfunction, blood pressure, muscle strength, fatigue, and chronic pain, as well as stress and anxiety. Because it is a gentle mind-body exercise, tai chi is ideal for older people or those who have moderate levels of physical ability. You can find dozens of easy tutorials online to follow anywhere or look for a dojo in your area.

GET
NUTTY

Trees are one of our great resources, offering shade from the sun's heat and wood for fires when it's cold. They clear the air, provide homes for birds and animals, and give us leaves for fertilizer. They also offer delicious and healthful nuts to enjoy.

You can reduce your risk of heart disease just by having a serving of nuts five times per week. The high amount of unsaturated fat helps lower the LDL ("bad" cholesterol) and increase the HDL ("good" cholesterol) in your blood. The omega-3 fatty acids are absorbed by the LDL particles, which triggers the liver cells to remove this cholesterol from your blood.

DO NECK ROLLS
AT YOUR DESK

Many of us spend more hours at our computers than we do in our beds. If your daytime territory is mostly limited to a desk, make the best of it.

Periodically stop what you're doing and release the tension in your neck that builds up during long periods of working. Drop your head forward loosely, then slowly roll it to the right and back. Continue making a circle with your head, letting it drop toward your back and then to the left. Allow your head to fall forward, so your chin touches your collarbones, then repeat the circle. Do this three times slowly in a clockwise direction. Then reverse and roll in a counterclockwise direction.

TREAT YOUR SKIN
WITH CEDAR OIL

The cedar tree has a long and mystical history; its value is described in religious texts and poetry. The Arabs believed the cedars of Lebanon embodied a power that made them live forever. The ancient Egyptians used cedar resin in the process of mummification. Various cultures and spiritual traditions use cedar in rituals and ceremonies. It can also offer healing benefits for your body.

Aromatic cedar oil can aid oily skin, psoriasis, acne, and other skin conditions. Blend a few drops in a carrier oil such as grape seed, jojoba, or olive oil and apply it to improve skin quality. You can also use it as a massage oil—its warming quality can ease arthritic joints.

BREAK UP
YOUR WORKOUT

You may be able to accomplish more today if you take it little by little, instead of letting the enormity of the day's demands overwhelm you. Stress and boredom often result from trying to handle too much. Try breaking up your day into manageable portions.

If you tend to get bored or tired during a long workout, try doing smaller amounts of exercise several times a day. Take a short walk before work. Take the stairs rather than the elevator. Do some yoga in the evening to release the stress of the day. Plan a routine that works best for you.

SWITCH TO
GLASS CONTAINERS

There is more to glass than meets the eye. Not only is it beautiful and functional; glass may provide healing as well. Today, look more carefully at the potential benefits of glass.

Plastic containers may increase your chances of getting certain types of cancer, according to the Canadian group Environmental Defence and acknowledged by the US National Toxicology Program. A toxic chemical compound called bisphenol A (BPA), used in many plastics, can leech into food. Switch to glass bottles and storage containers for food, and don't heat plastic in the microwave.

TREAT YOURSELF
TO SCENTED SOAP

Be good to yourself today. Too often we deny ourselves little luxuries because we think they're extravagances. Many small treats don't cost much, however, and they provide a great deal of pleasure. Go ahead and splurge a little—you're worth it!

Any kind of soap will clean your body, but aromatherapy soap heightens your senses, influences your mood, and adds a touch of elegance to your daily ritual. Buy hand-milled soaps made from natural ingredients and scented with pure essential oils. To perk up body *and* mind in the morning, wash with mint-scented soap. To ease your muscles in the evening, try a lavender-scented soap.

UP YOUR OMEGA-3S

Your diet and lifestyle affect not only how long you live, but your quality of life as well. The right nutrients can have you feeling your best, while nutrient deficiencies can lead to discomfort or even serious illness.

Augment your well-being by taking an omega-3 supplement. These fatty acids possess a natural anti-inflammatory, reducing the risk of inflammatory conditions such as rheumatoid arthritis and fibromyalgia, as well as symptoms like joint pain and fatigue. You can also add more omega-3s to your diet by eating certain fish, such as bluefish, herring, mackerel, salmon, sardines, and tuna.

FIND EXCUSES
TO EXERCISE

You've heard the saying "Life is what you make of it." Today, make the most of those ordinary moments that you usually waste. The key is to stay attentive and enrich your appreciation of the possibilities available in your daily life.

Your daily routine and activities offer plenty of opportunities for sneaking in exercise. For instance, take the stairs instead of the elevator. Do semi-squats while you are waiting on hold. Position your phone a distance from your desk so you have to get up to answer it. Rake leaves rather than blowing them away.

CHANGE YOUR
DAILY ROUTINE

Energy, motivation, and ultimately productivity drop when you become physically dulled by doing the same things over and over. Today, make some healthy changes in your routine.

When you shower, wash yourself in a different order than usual—if you generally start on your left side, begin on your right. If you normally sleep on the right side of the bed, sleep on the left. When you're ready, attempt some bigger changes to push your adaptability, boost your energy, and feel reinvigorated.

SING

Your voice is a wonderful gift. With it, you communicate with those around you, deepening bonds and expressing your own thoughts and feelings. It also gives you the ability to say it in song.

Singing can heal, whether you sing in the shower, the church choir, or on karaoke night. Singing eases stress, reduces blood pressure, and slows heart rate. A three-year study at the Levine School of Music in Washington, DC, found that seniors who sang in a chorus had fewer doctors' visits, experienced less depression, and needed less medication. A study at Goethe University in Germany showed that singing improved immunity. Pick a favorite song and start singing!

PICK UP TRASH
WHEN YOU WALK

If we don't care for our environment, it can't take care of us. Our quality of life depends on the quality of our planet; our health depends on its health. Today, be aware of how your actions impact the earth and do your part to lessen the burden—every little thing counts.

Combine environmental consciousness with exercise. When you go for a walk or hike, take a bag with you and pick up trash along the way. If you walk every day and fill a bag at a time, you'll soon see a noticeable improvement. All that bending over helps work your waistline and stretch out your hamstrings too.

TRY HAND REFLEXOLOGY

Treat your hands kindly. They are one of the most important and amazingly intricate parts of your body. They help you experience each day: feeding and dressing you, touching a loved one, working on a favorite hobby, and so much more.

Usually we think of reflexology as a type of foot massage, but your hands have reflexology points on them too. According to this holistic healing modality, each part of your hands relates to another part of your body. The fingers link to the head and neck, the middle of the palm to the torso, and the part near the wrist to the lower sections of your body. Massaging points on your hand can aid problems in many different parts of your body.

PARK
FAR AWAY

Find opportunities to get healthy wherever you go. Your daily activities provide possibilities for well-being, in a relatively painless and practical way. Every little bit helps!

When you go to the mall or the supermarket, park your car at the far end of the lot. That way you'll incorporate extra exercise into your shopping trip. If you weigh 160 pounds, you'll burn about 85 calories per mile walking at a moderate pace and more if you walk faster. Walking also improves circulation, respiration, and muscle tone.

EAT
SEA VEGETABLES

Perhaps we feel drawn to the sea because it is our mother, the source from which humankind emerged countless millennia ago. Or maybe it is because our bodies are largely composed of slightly salty water. Whatever the reason, you can draw nourishment from the sea.

Sea vegetables contain vitamins A, B complex, C, and E, as well as the fifty-six minerals and trace minerals your body requires to function properly. They also have very little fat, a plus for those trying to maintain a healthy weight. Try arame, kelp, dulse, kombu, nori, and/or wakame in soups, stir-fry, and sushi.

OPEN YOUR WINDOWS

Become aware of the air you breathe, without which you would soon cease to exist. As yoga postulates, through breath work you can reconnect to your body and promote better health.

Whether at home, in your car, or in your office, make sure your space is well ventilated. Open the windows whenever possible and consider exhaust fans or air-to-air heat-exchanging devices for your home or workspace that draw fresh air in through one duct and expel it out through another. Make sure stoves and heaters in your home vent outdoors. Fresh air is shown to improve blood pressure and heart rate, strengthen the immune system, and clean your lungs.

REACH OUT AND
TOUCH SOMEONE

As electronic media become more popular, many of us have lost the personal touch. *Facebook* and text messages are no substitute for real human contact; try getting up close and personal.

Touch close friends and family members frequently. According to the Touch Research Institute at the University of Miami Miller School of Medicine, touch can ease pain, reduce stress, boost immunity, help premature babies thrive, help wounds heal faster, and aid in reducing a range of diseases, from diabetes to cancer. Even a stranger's friendly touch, such as brushing a cashier's finger when you receive change, can have positive effects.

TRY A NEW TYPE OF WORKOUT

Exercise is a task many of us are less than enthusiastic about, and the motivation can quickly decline even further when we become stuck in one dull workout routine. It's time to revamp your regimen and bust out of that bored rut.

Vary your workout program by checking out an online class or signing up with a friend for something new and different in your area. Most fitness and sports centers offer lots of different programs. How about barre or Pilates? Kickboxing or karate? Zumba or belly dancing? You'll notice that you use muscles you don't ordinarily use in your familia routine. You might really enjoy it too. The only way to find out if you like something is by giving it a try!

EAT TO A MORE YOUTHFUL YOU

Aging is a fact of life, but it is also what you make of it. No matter what your age, value it and make the most of it. Each time of life offers unique possibilities. Cherish them.

Add foods with antioxidants to your diet to help you enjoy doing the things you want to do. A diet high in antioxidants has a direct correlation to reduced age-related mental and physical degeneration, according to the US Department of Agriculture's Jean Mayer Human Nutrition Research Center on Aging, based at Tufts University. Many fruits and vegetables, including berries, broccoli, tomatoes, and spinach, contain antioxidants, and can be packed for an easy on-the-go boost. You can also find antioxidant supplements online and in most health food stores.

DO THE
TWIST

Staying active is essential in order to stay limber. If you don't exercise your body, it will stagnate like a body of water blocked with debris. Fortunately, there are easy ways to stay flexible—wherever you are.

Loosen up periodically while sitting at your desk or on your couch, or while out and about. Twist as far as you can to your left, holding on to the back and arm of your chair for leverage if seated. Hold this position for a count of fifteen, then slowly unwind. Then do the same thing, turning to your right. Repeat this three times every hour to keep your back, neck, and shoulders limber and relieve muscular strain.

PART 3
SPIRIT

LIFT YOUR SPIRITS
WITH ROSE QUARTZ

When you think happy thoughts, you feel better. When you dwell on problems and what's wrong in the world, your sense of well-being spirals downward. Research shows that positive thinking can help you improve your health and maintain a strong connection to the world around you.

Healers who work with crystals say rose quartz emits gentle, uplifting vibrations that can boost your spirits. Carry a small piece of smooth, tumbled rose quartz in your pocket and rub it often to encourage a sense of joy and inner peace.

PROTECT YOUR HOME WITH AN EYE AMULET

Most of us see only a portion of what exists around us. The tendency to restrict our visual awareness has increased with the proliferation of personal electronic devices. Open your eyes to the powers that be.

The ancient Turks and Greeks believed in the curse of the "evil eye" and used eye amulets to guard against it. Often these amulets consisted of concentric circles rendered in dark blue, light blue, and white that resemble eyes. Hang one near the entrance to your home to repel unwanted energies.

ENCOURAGE SOMEONE'S
SPIRITUAL GROWTH

Today, nurture a loved one's spirit. Notice how lifting another person up boosts your own sense of well-being too. Being a part of someone's spiritual journey also strengthens your bond with them and can inspire new spiritual growth within yourself as well.

Instead of forcing your ideas on someone else, encourage them to seek out answers independently. Whether or not you are religiously oriented, you can nurture someone's search for truth, perhaps by presenting various options and opinions. Trust that a loved one will find the right path for them.

MAKE AN OFFERING

Today, set an intention to be content with your life, just as it is right now. Instead of worrying about little annoyances or thinking about what you lack, focus on the good things in your life.

One way to show gratitude—and continue the cycle of abundance—is to make an offering to a deity of your choice. Write a short prayer, like a spiritual thank-you note, to your favorite god, goddess, angel, or spirit. You can read it out loud or silently, visualizing that deity receiving your offering of thanks with joy.

GET ANSWERS WITH A PENDULUM

Starting something new can be refreshing to the spirit—no wonder we use the phrase "a fresh start." If something in your life isn't working for you—a job, a relationship, a habit—staying in that rut probably won't make things better. Instead, try a different tactic: Start over.

If you're uncertain about your direction, you can use a pendulum to get answers. Either purchase a pendulum or make one by hanging a light weight of some kind on a chain. Hold the chain loosely, letting the bob dangle, and ask a yes or no question. Let the pendulum swing without trying to move it. A side-to-side motion means "no" and a back-and-forth motion means "yes."

CLEANSE YOUR ENERGY FIELD WITH PERIDOT

Crystal workers attribute healing properties to various stones and use them to aid many spiritual conditions. Meditating with, contemplating, or just carrying a certain crystal on your person can heal and elevate your spirit—and even manifest your desires. Originally, birthstones were worn to attract wanted qualities and ameliorate unwanted ones.

Since ancient times, peridot has been considered to have cleansing and protective properties. Wear or carry this stone to help you release negative emotions such as jealousy, resentment, anger, and stress that can weigh down your spirit and leave you with a sense of unease.

INCREASE THE SWEETNESS IN YOUR LIFE

We've been taught to value hard work and sacrifice, while looking skeptically at pleasure. However, the Law of Attraction suggests we should do otherwise. It tells us that when we feel good, our energy level increases, and so does our ability to create the lives we desire.

Our cravings for sweets can be an indication that we seek more sweetness in our lives spiritually. Do you feel a lack of love and joy? Does your life seem more bitter than sweet? Giving what you wish to receive is the first step. Find ways to share sweetness with others—gifting a friend their favorite chocolates, hugging a sibling, smiling at people you pass on the street—and you'll find more coming back.

TAP THE
POWER OF THREE

The opposite of growth and change is stagnation. Once you stop expanding your horizons you face the prospect of deterioration spiritually. Today, push through any stagnant energy and revitalize your spirit.

In numerology, feng shui, tarot, and other metaphysical schools of thought, the number three represents growth and actualization. You can invite growth into your home or place of business by grouping objects in combinations of three. Position furnishings, artwork, plants, and candles in this arrangement.

SWITCH UP
YOUR ARTWORK

Sometimes you just need to stir things up a bit to keep life interesting and encourage new perspectives. A change of pace. A change of scenery. A change of décor.

Museums frequently rearrange the artwork they display in order to increase interest for visitors. You can too. Move around the pictures in your home or office and hang them in different locations. You'll see them in a different light, literally. Change the photographs you display too—including the ones on your phone lock screen and phone and computer backgrounds. Update them with more current photos.

USE AFFIRMATIONS TO INCREASE YOUR PROSPERITY

Prosperity is both a state of mind and a state of being. If you're not as prosperous as you'd like to be, it's time to examine your attitude and increase your abundance.

An affirmation is a short, positive statement you use to change your thinking or behavior, and to produce something you desire. Create a prosperity affirmation, such as "I now open myself to receive prosperity of all kinds," and repeat it often throughout the day. You can also write your affirmation on sticky notes to post in places where you will see them regularly—such as a bathroom mirror or your car's dashboard—so you remember to recite it.

OBSERVE SIGNS FROM THE UNIVERSE

Many important discoveries and experiences in our lives come to us seemingly by chance. Scientific "accidents" have brought us numerous things of great value, including penicillin and X-rays. Today, allow yourself to be guided by serendipitous occurrences—you may find something wonderful happens.

Start noticing signs. Finding a penny on the street could mean you'll soon receive money. A strong urge to call someone you haven't seen in a while could mean that person is thinking about you too. Hunches and coincidences may indicate that the universe is communicating with you.

ENGAGE IN
SPIRITUAL SHARING

Care for yourself and your loved ones today by engaging in a sharing activity. Togetherness creates positive bonds that can translate into good health and a better sense of well-being. For example, the Center on Addiction found that teens who regularly eat dinner with family members have a lower risk of substance abuse.

If you and a loved one follow a certain faith, attend a place of worship together. If you don't subscribe to a particular religion, you can still engage in spiritual sharing. Say a nondenominational prayer before a meal. Visit a sacred historic site together. Meditate side by side. Watch a documentary about a religion in a foreign country and discuss it.

MEDITATE ON THE CHARIOT CARD

Continual demands may have you racing to resolve every crisis. You have no time to relax or do the things you really want to do. Take care of yourself by turning over the reins for once. Allow someone—or something—to help out and shoulder the burden.

From a tarot deck, select The Chariot card. It usually depicts a person driving a chariot drawn by two creatures, one black and one white. The card represents steering a steady course and constructively handling multiple factors in your life. Meditate on this card to resolve conflicts and achieve self-mastery.

LISTEN TO
WIND CHIMES

Like any muscle, the brain improves when you exercise it. Beyond sharpening the mind, practicing methods for stimulating your gray matter can spark deeper thoughts that nourish spiritual growth and open up your subconscious.

Listening to the pleasing sound of wind chimes can soothe and relax your mind, allowing you to access more of the intuitive part of your brain. The lack of a symmetrical tune or rhythm prevents your logical brain from trying to make sense of the sounds. In feng shui, the ancient Chinese art of placement, wind chimes are used to clear energetic blockages and to gently stimulate activity in all areas of life.

CONSULT
THE *I CHING*

Many spiritual teachers espouse the benefits of focusing on the present and letting the future come about as it will. What you do today lays the foundation for what will evolve into the future. Therefore, by giving this day, this moment, the proper attention, you take care of tomorrow.

The three-thousand-year-old oracle known as the *I Ching* offers wise counsel when you need answers. Also known as the *Book of Changes*, it contains sixty-four hexagrams (six-lined patterns) that represent different approaches to problem-solving. You can find the *I Ching* online, download an ebook version, or purchase a physical copy to keep on hand.

PRACTICE NONVIOLENCE

The boundaries between you and other people are what prevents your spirit from connecting completely to the world around you. Today, try focusing on your commonality rather than your differences. You can acknowledge differences without letting them stand between you. Fear, isolation, and prejudice have a detrimental effect on us as individuals and societies.

Practicing nonviolence is an act of strength, not weakness. Nonviolence is much more than not harming another person physically. It means monitoring your thoughts and feelings too. Thinking hateful thoughts can have a destructive effect, and so can venting angry emotions in unhealthy ways. Challenge these thoughts and explore better ways to release anger. You may want to buy products from companies that support peace efforts too, rather than those that profit from war.

PROTECT YOURSELF
WITH AMBER

What strategies do you have in place for protection? You may not be able to ward off danger at every corner, but some simple practices can make you more secure. It's better to be safe than sorry, as the old saying goes.

For centuries, amber has been linked with protection. Use this hardened resin to safeguard yourself, whether driving to work, traveling to an unfamiliar location, or facing a fear. Purchase a few amber beads and string them on a piece of jeweler's wire. Then attach the beads to the rearview mirror inside your car, store them in your workbag or luggage, or adorn your wrist with them. You can also carry a chunk of amber.

CHOOSE A PERSONAL SYMBOL

Symbols, both natural and human-made, abound in our world. In modern society, businesses use symbols called logos to express a company's intention. Consider some well-known symbols: What impressions do they evoke in you?

Choose a symbol that holds cultural or spiritual significance for you. This symbol can serve as a touchstone and provide a sense of connection or comfort. Draw it on paper, carve it in wood, or have a jeweler craft it in silver or gold. Whenever you see or touch your symbol, you'll feel an inner connection to something larger than yourself.

CHART YOUR POWER DAYS

We never know how long we have on the planet or what lies ahead. Therefore, it makes sense to enjoy each day to the fullest, and to take advantage of the opportunities that come your way.

Astrologers say you have at least twelve days each year that are especially auspicious. Known as power days, they fall each month on the same date as your birthday. If you were born on the eighteenth of a month, for example, the eighteenth day of every month is a power day for you. Seize the potential of these fortunate dates.

IMPRINT WATER WITH YOUR INTENTIONS

Your mind is a powerful magnet that can attract anything you desire. With just a word or phrase, even spoken only in your own head, you can use this inner power to draw something to you. Like attracts like.

Words impact the molecular nature of water, according to research done by Japanese scientist Masaru Emoto. Write a word that encapsulates what you seek, such as *love, peace,* or *health*, on a piece of paper and tape it to a bottle of water, with the word facing in. The energy of the word imprints the water with positive vibrations. Drink the water to ingest those good vibes and manifest your desire.

DO SOMETHING CHILDISH

Lighten up today! Spiritual teachers emphasize the benefits of laughter and childlike joy. In the Bible's Gospel of Matthew, Jesus says, "The Kingdom of heaven belongs to those who are like these children." Try to approach life with an open heart and a playful mind—you may experience unexpected blessings.

Recall something you enjoyed doing as a child, such as blowing soap bubbles, flying a kite, or splashing about in mud puddles. Let the child in you come out and play again. Engage in one of those youthful expressions of joy. Don't censor or judge yourself—laugh at yourself instead. Notice how quickly your spirits lift.

CONTACT
AN ANGEL

When the Spanish conquerors sailed to what's now South America, the indigenous people couldn't see their ships because they had no conception of such things. Likewise, most of us don't see angels, ghosts, and other spirits because we aren't open to seeing them. What would happen if you let go of preconceptions such as these?

Some sources say all you have to do is ask the angel to make itself known to you. Then, listen. You may want to contact a specific guardian angel for guidance, such as Jophiel the angel of wisdom, or reach out to an ancestor or loved one who has passed on to offer thanks for their role in your life.

SEEK HELP FROM
YOUR SPIRIT ANIMAL

Animals are a big part of the world around us. After all, we are just one of an estimated two million species. There is much to learn from animals; their ties to the physical and ethereal realms extend deep within the teachings and traditions of numerous cultures past and present.

In shamanic traditions, spirit animals serve as guides and helpers to those of us here on earth. Do you feel an affinity with a particular animal? That may be your spirit animal or totem. When you need assistance with a life challenge or seek guidance, ask your spirit animal to lend you its special characteristics. You can also get a free reading online to determine your spirit animal or discover what animal you should draw power and insight from on a given day.

LOOK FOR AURAS

Today, sharpen your observation skills in order to understand people and situations more clearly. As eyewitness studies have shown, most of us only partially see what's going on around us. How much do *you* miss every day?

Your emotions, mental state, and physical health are all reflected in your aura—the subtle energy field that surrounds your physical body. An aura may look like a whitish or colored glow extending about six inches or more out from the body. Although most people don't notice auras, you can gain information about someone by learning to see them. Practice seeing the auras around other people—it's easier if the person is in front of a dark or white background.

PACK A
TRAVEL ALTAR

In recent years, travel has become more stressful than ever. High costs, delays, security checks, and crowds can diminish the joys of a journey—if you let them. Whether you're going to a foreign land or taking a day trip, see traveling as a chance to expand your horizons, literally and figuratively.

When you travel, bring sacred items with you to create a portable altar that will help you feel serene and openhearted wherever you are. Pack a few items in a padded cosmetic bag: a small candle, a cone of your favorite incense, a quartz crystal, or a figurine of a beloved deity. Wrap them up in a scarf that can double as an altar cloth. When you get to your accommodations, conduct a settling-in ritual.

WEAR YELLOW TOPAZ FOR CONFIDENCE

As a personal quality, confidence is like a superpower: It imparts strength wherever strength is needed. And the best thing about this superpower is that we all have access to it.

Crystal workers link the yellow topaz gemstone with self-confidence and leadership. To overcome self-doubt or uncertainty, wear this golden crystal as a necklace, bracelet, or ring. Alternatively, you can carry a piece of yellow topaz in your pocket. It helps you express your inner power, tap your personal resources, and attract fortunate opportunities.

FOLLOW
MERCURY

We tend to get sucked into our own little worlds. There is just so much to think about and do each day, that it's hard to point blame for forgetting that there is more to life than ourselves. But there is so much we are missing out on when our view is this narrow—including what lies beyond our own planet. The universe is infinite, and its many stars and planets can expand our understanding of ourselves in unexpected ways.

Astrologers link the planet Mercury with our internal processes. About every four months, for a period of several weeks at a time, Mercury appears to move backward (or retrograde) in its path around the sun. During these times, your intuition and communications may be less clear than usual, resulting in mistakes or confusion. Check Mercury's position before making important decisions.

LIFT YOUR SPIRITS WITH GRAPEFRUIT

Low in calories and high in vitamins A and C, beta-carotene, and lycopene, grapefruit has a lot to offer your health—inside and out. A cross between the orange and pomelo, this tart pink fruit is often overlooked for its sweeter counterparts, but not today.

The clean, refreshing scent of grapefruit essential oil can lift your spirits and help counteract feelings of discouragement. Put a few drops on a clean handkerchief and inhale the aroma to ease your nerves and invite a sense of peace. If you're feeling lethargic or apathetic, sniff grapefruit to wake up your enthusiasm. Consider diffusing the scent in your living space or placing a grapefruit air freshener in your car to utilize its healing powers regularly.

TAP
IN TO ESP

Numerous studies have linked electromagnetic fields (EMFs) with health risks, including leukemia, brain tumors, and chronic fatigue. The Environmental Protection Agency suggests there is reason for concern. You can't avoid all EMFs, but you may be able to reduce your risk and take some time to recharge away from your phone screen with an alternate method of communication.

Try sending a friend a message using only your mind. Extrasensory perception (ESP) is immediate and knows no boundaries. If you find yourself thinking about someone you haven't been in communication with lately, that person may be trying to contact you.

SEND POSITIVE ENERGY TO YOUR SKIN

Beauty is more than skin deep, but keeping your skin looking beautiful can help you feel better about yourself in every way. Take the time to treat your skin well and feel the revitalizing effects on your spirit.

Close your eyes and rub your palms together vigorously. Then hold your hands up about six inches in front of your face, with your palms facing you. Imagine positive energy flowing from your hands to your face, rejuvenating and refreshing your skin. See imperfections disappearing. Envision your skin glowing with good health.

CONTEMPLATE
THE LOTUS SYMBOL

Until the latter half of the last century, most Westerners were unaware of Tibet's rich spiritual, cultural, and healing traditions. The three-thousand-year-old mind-body-spirit practice of Tibetan medicine is now available throughout the United States. It emphasizes balance, natural remedies, and energetic harmony.

In Tibetan Buddhism, the lotus symbolizes enlightenment. Because this beautiful flower grows from the mud at the bottom of a swamp, the lotus represents the ability to transcend the muck of everyday life to attain a heightened state of clarity. Tibetan art often depicts the Buddha seated on a lotus flower. Contemplate the symbol to help you rise above destructive thoughts and emotions and elevate your intuition.

REMOVE COMPUTER STRESS WITH TOURMALINE

Stress and the countless effects it can have on our mental and physical health rob us of the ability to find happiness in our lives. The anxiety, aches and pains, and more leave little room to focus on anything else. They can also isolate us from others, and place strain on current relationships. Stressors are omnipresent in modern life, but you can choose how you react to them.

Place a piece of black tourmaline beside your work and/or home computer. This crystal is a powerful energy balancer. It helps protect you from the adverse effects of electromagnetic stress that can come from computers, Wi-Fi, cell phones, and other electronic equipment. It blocks bad vibes and strengthens your aura.

HEAL
OLD WOUNDS

Spiritual self-care isn't just about developing your beliefs surrounding a higher power or specific faith tradition. It's also about expanding and strengthening your relationships with others, especially those closest to you. Opening up to your partner about your feelings is one of the best ways to become closer to one another. However, true intimacy requires a willingness to be vulnerable and to trust that your partner won't hurt you or let you down—things that don't come naturally to many, especially those who have been hurt in the past.

In meditation, contemplate an old hurt that still triggers anger, sadness, or other unwanted emotions. Try to recover the memory of how that wound originated. Envision the person who first hurt you. Visualize a beam of pink light running between your heart and that person's heart, softening the old pain.

OPEN YOUR
THIRD EYE

Open your mind and heart today in order to see the world around you more clearly. This may also mean seeing yourself more clearly. Often, we deny or overlook things that we don't want to acknowledge or deal with. Don't let conditioning or fear keep you blinded now.

Close your physical eyes and turn your inner attention to the brow or third eye chakra. This energy center is located between your eyebrows, where your nose joins your forehead. Imagine indigo-colored light glowing there. This practice helps to increase your intuition and insight.

CONTEMPLATE THE STRENGTH CARD

Whether you are hoping to better connect with your community, expand your knowledge of a certain faith, or reexamine your beliefs around a higher power, you need endurance to reach your goal. Today, work on building spiritual strength at a pace that's comfortable for you; proceeding in a slow and steady manner may prevent setbacks or burnout.

One of the twenty-two cards in the tarot's Major Arcana, Strength usually depicts a young woman holding the jaws of a lion. The card's message is to gain mastery over your ego and the animal nature using patience, gentleness, and compassion. Use this card as a meditation aid to gain inner strength.

EXPLORE THE SPACE
BETWEEN BREATHS

A butterfly must beat its wings against the walls of its cocoon in order to develop the strength to fly. So, too, must we encounter adversity in our lives in order to grow strong. Today, see the challenges facing you as tools for personal growth—like experiential free weights that build your life muscles.

When you feel overwhelmed or burdened by problems, allow your awareness to dive deeply into the space between your in-breaths and out-breaths. This is a potent place of stillness and calm, a place without boundaries. If you allow your mind to formulate a clear question now, you may receive an inspired, intuitive answer.

GAZE INTO YOUR
LOVED ONE'S EYES

It may not be possible to totally escape heartbreak or unhappiness in your relationships, but love should bring you more happiness than sorrow. If you are feeling disconnected from your partner, due to an argument or external stressors, it is time to give your bond a bit of extra TLC.

Look deeply into each other's eyes and allow loving feelings to expand within you. Sense the connection between you—you may feel an energetic exchange. Open yourself to the other person's gaze, trying not to hold anything back. Notice any insights that arise into your awareness.

SMILE INWARDLY

Stress causes us to tighten everything from our muscles to our behaviors and attitudes. To help beat stress today, choose to loosen up in spirit. See how much better it feels to be flexible instead of tense.

Close your eyes and smile. Feel yourself growing more relaxed and at ease. After a few moments, turn the smile inward at yourself. Sense yourself being warmed inside by the love and beauty of your smile. Let go of all stress and rigidity and just be.

MAKE A TALISMAN

Your soul is the body and mind's command center. Therefore, your spiritual state and the relationships you have with yourself and the world around you will have an impact on every area of your life.

Talismans are good-luck charms you make to attract something you want. In a drawstring pouch, place several small items that symbolize whatever it is you wish to attract, be it new friendships, more self-confidence, or a sense of peace. These things should all hold positive significance for you. When you've finished, affirm to yourself that what you desire is coming to you now.

CONSULT
THE RUNES

Seek the wisdom of stones today. Stones are among the most ancient substances on earth and have many stories to tell. They teach geologists about the past and reveal the future to seers.

The rune system derives from old Norse alphabets and equates each letter symbol with a meaning. Casting runes is a form of divination that can be used to find answers to your questions. Early rune symbols were carved on stones, bones, and wood. Today they may be imprinted in gemstones, glass, plastic, clay, or other substances. They are easy to carry with you anywhere, and you can even download a rune app on your smartphone to cast the stones with a simple click.

TAP IN TO THE
ENERGY OF MARS

Courage, confidence, enthusiasm—these are all traits that build on your zest for life, but they can also ebb and flow as frequently as the tides. One small setback or fear can derail your motivation or zap your self-esteem. Today, take a small, flavorful step toward restoring your belief in yourself and pushing past obstacles.

Since antiquity, herbalists have linked plants with planetary influences and prescribed herbal remedies that contained the energies of the planets. Mars is the planet of courage, vitality, and assertiveness. According to some herbalists, you can harness the motivating energy of Mars by ingesting herbs and plants with Martian qualities, especially spiciness: cayenne pepper, hot mustard, salsa, horseradish, and curry.

LISTEN TO
YOUR BACK

In the daily rush to get things done, a lot can go unnoticed—even in our own bodies. With so much to do and so little time in the day to do it, it can be easy to overlook or even ignore aches and pains, hunger and thirst, and more. But through those physical twinges and soreness, our bodies may be communicating deeper issues; it's important to pay attention.

In her bestselling book *You Can Heal Your Life,* Louise Hay links back problems with problems in the psyche. Money woes are associated with lower back pain. Guilt can cause problems in the midback. Feeling unloved may manifest in the upper back. Tune in to how your back feels in this moment and consider whether it is trying to tell you something. Design positive affirmations to help correct these issues.

HEAL YOUR HEART
WITH RUBY IN ZOISITE

When a relationship ends, be it with a friend, significant other, or business partner, grief is normal. But the end of a relationship isn't the end of the world. Instead of languishing in misery, it's important to take positive steps to heal this wound in order to embrace new possibilities in the future.

The red ruby, associated with passion, and the green zoisite, linked with temperance, balance one another to ease feelings of grief. Wear the gem near your heart to bring painful emotions to the surface where they can be healed. This stone helps you understand the meaning behind loss and lets you evolve beyond suffering.

USE THE LOVERS CARD TO ENHANCE INTIMACY

Take a simple step to improve your sex life today. Many health professionals now recommend having sex often as a way to improve your overall well-being. Sex releases feel-good chemicals in your brain and increases life satisfaction by fulfilling the deep human desire for connection.

Among the twenty-two cards in the tarot's Major Arcana you'll find The Lovers. This card symbolizes the union of male and female, and some decks, such as The Gilded Tarot, depict beautiful erotic imagery. To encourage intimacy with a partner, place the card on your bedside table or another place in your bedroom where you'll see it often.

LEARN ABOUT
YOUR SUN SIGN

Today, appreciate the sun, the center around which our solar system revolves. Nothing we know would exist without it. Early people revered the sun as a god. Welcome the roles the sun plays in your life.

When someone asks "What's your sign?" they mean "What part of the zodiac was the sun in when you were born?" For thousands of years, astrologers have studied the relationship between the positions of the heavenly bodies and events on earth. Consult astrology websites or read a book on the subject to learn more about your strengths, weaknesses, and possibilities.

INVITE A
DEITY'S BLESSING

The benefits of spirituality have been well documented by numerous clinical studies. Cultivating spiritual growth can eliminate stress, reduce depression, improve social bonds, and so much more. Today, strengthen your connection to a higher power.

Invite a deity to bless the different parts of your life. In your yard or garden, place a statue of your favorite spiritual figure, such as the Buddha, the Virgin Mary, the Green Man, or a guardian angel. Or set one by your front door to welcome family members and visitors to your home. Carry a miniature version of the deity with you when you travel, display it in your office space, or keep it in your car's glove box.

EXAMINE YOUR HEART LINES

No matter how long you've known someone, you can never know everything about him or her—and the mystery is part of the appeal. However, learning to appreciate something about your beloved that you may have overlooked can be a tantalizing experience. Try a new way to open up a bit more to your partner and invite them to open up more to you.

A person's hand contains a wealth of information—if you know what to look for. The heart line is the middle line on most people's palms, which runs horizontally from the space between the thumb and index finger toward the outside of the palm. If it's straight, that person is a pragmatist; if it dips down toward the wrist, that person is a romantic.

SILENTLY
BLESS OTHERS

Charitable acts benefit the giver at least as much as they do the recipient. In his book *The Healing Power of Doing Good*, Allan Luks, former executive director of Big Brothers Big Sisters of New York City, concluded that "helping contributes to the maintenance of good health, and it can diminish the effect of diseases and disorders both serious and minor, psychological and physical."

Sending good thoughts and blessings to others is an act of kindness. Thoughts and feelings resonate energy, and that energy affects you as well as everyone else. Even if someone angers you—especially if someone angers you—bless that person instead of cursing them. Kindness begets kindness.

GET DAILY E-INSPIRATION

Give yourself the consideration you would offer to your dearest friend. If you tend to overlook yourself and your own needs, while tending to the needs of others, it's time to stop shortchanging yourself. Treat yourself to some TLC regularly.

Begin each day on a positive note. Sign up to receive inspirational quotes daily by email—you'll find lots of Internet sites that provide this service. Every day when you turn on your computer, you'll be treated to upbeat and heartwarming sayings.

ATTEND AN UNFAMILIAR RITUAL OR CEREMONY

Indulge your curiosity today and expand your horizons by delving into something completely unknown. When you were a kid, everything was new and exciting. Recapture that youthful enthusiasm. Usually the only way to learn if you like something is by trying it.

Regardless of whether you are the religious type, you can benefit from the uplifting aspects of spiritual rituals. Attend a ritual or ceremony associated with a belief system about which you know little or nothing: Wicca, Hinduism, Islam, or something else. Open your heart and mind to the experience.

INDEX

Abundance, 59, 121, 127
Acupressure, 67
Acupuncture, 29
Affirmations, 127, 156, 159
Aging, slowing, 74, 94, 114
Aloe vera, 90
Altar, portable, 142
Amber, 134
Amen, Daniel G., 58
Amulets, 119
Angels, 121, 139, 163
Animals, spirit, 140
Animals, support, 40
Answers, finding, 120, 122, 132, 153, 157
Anti-inflammatory agents, 94, 103
Antioxidants, 70, 114
Anxiety, calming, 19, 27, 38, 92, 96, 149. *See also* Stress
Arguments, avoiding, 34, 89, 154
Aromatherapy, 28, 102
Artwork, 125, 126
Astrology, 36, 136, 144, 158, 162
Attention span, increasing, 42, 57
Attraction, law of, 53, 124
Auras, 141, 149
Awareness, 119, 153, 154

Bach, Edward, 92
Balance, restoring, 75, 86, 88, 96
Battles, choosing, 34
Beliefs, 69, 167
Black currant seed oil, 94
Blessings, 156, 163, 165
Blood pressure, lowering, 70, 96, 106, 111

Body
  exercise for, 83, 100, 104, 113, 115
  foods for, 66, 68, 79, 84, 97, 103, 110, 114, 145
  harmonizing, 81
  listening to, 87
  self-care activities for, 65–115
  vitamins for, 74, 110, 145
Book of Changes, 132
Boundaries, 19, 133
Brain
  balancing hemispheres, 44
  exercising, 24, 35, 58, 63, 131
  improving, 24, 42, 48, 58, 131
Breathing techniques, 44, 85, 111
Buddha, 148, 163

Calendula cream, 82
Campbell, Joseph, 23
Cancer, 101, 112, 146
Car scents, 28
Cedar oil, 99
Ceremonies, 99, 167
Chakras, 75, 91, 151
Challenges, 14, 17, 73, 153. *See also* Stress
Charms, 156
Chi, 96
Childlike joy, 138
Circulation, improving, 68, 80, 91, 109
Color Me Beautiful, 37
Colors, 37, 54, 62
Computer stress, 67, 98, 149. *See also* Stress

Confidence, 37, 45, 80, 95, 143, 156, 158
Consumerism, 51
Courage, 73, 80, 158
Courses, 35, 45, 113
Creativity
  expressing, 21, 31, 41
  increasing, 57, 80, 83
  relaxation and, 60
Crystals/stones
  amber, 134
  birthstones, 123
  black tourmaline, 149
  healing power of, 118, 123, 149, 160
  meditating with, 123
  peridot, 123
  quartz, 118, 142
  ruby, 160
  self-protection with, 134
  topaz, 143
  zoisite, 160

Dancing, 83
Daydreams, 53
Decisions, making, 14, 144
Decluttering tips, 51
Deities, 121, 142, 163. *See also* Gods
Detox, 29, 101
Diabetes, 71, 112
Digestion, aiding, 68
Dinners/meals, 68, 84, 129. *See also* Foods
Drumming, 78

Edison, Thomas, 17
Electromagnetic fields (EMFs), 146, 149

Emotions
  affecting decisions, 14
  colors influencing, 37, 54, 62
  impact of, 30, 87, 141
  releasing, 81, 123, 133, 150, 160
Emoto, Masaru, 137
Energy
  balancing, 88, 149
  boosting, 72, 78, 83, 85, 88, 124, 125, 158
  chakras, 75, 91, 151
  clearing, 75, 123, 131
  of Mars, 158
  negative energy, 119
  positive energy, 137, 147, 165
  yin and yang energies, 88
Environment, helping, 47, 101, 107, 146
Essential oils, 28, 42, 102, 145
Exercise/workouts
  dancing, 83
  excuses for avoiding, 104
  new exercises, 100, 113
  routine for, 100
  twists, 115
  varying, 100, 113
Exfoliation, 77
Explorations, 89
Extrasensory perception (ESP), 146

Fair trade purchases, 47
Family, 39, 112, 124, 129
Feelings, revealing, 30. *See also* Emotions
Feng shui, 29, 96, 125, 131
Finances, 59, 61
Fire, breath of, 85
Flowers, 62, 70, 82, 92, 148. *See also* Herbs

Focus
   balancing, 60, 86
   with dharana, 20
   on forgiveness, 27
   on present, 57, 132
   on priorities, 15, 20, 23, 32, 39, 51
Foods
   dinners/meals, 68, 84, 129
   fruits, 79, 114, 145
   nuts, 97
   omega-3s, 97, 103
   savoring, 66, 84
   vegetables, 79, 110, 114
Forgiveness, 27
Fresh air, 71, 111
Friendships, 25, 39, 62, 112, 124, 156, 160
Fruits, 79, 114, 145
Future, 132, 157, 160

Galilei, Galileo, 36
Gandhi, Mahatma, 71
Ginger, 68
Ginseng, 26
Glass containers, 101
Goals/dreams, 15, 17, 52, 53, 152
Gods/goddesses, 36, 46, 121, 162.
   See also Deities
Grapefruit, 145
Gratitude, expressing, 41, 51, 121
Grief, easing, 160

Hafiz, 48
Haiku, writing, 31
Hand reflexology, 108
Hands, observing, 164
Happiness
   animals and, 40

colors influencing, 37, 54, 62
increasing, 25, 32, 118, 124, 138, 154
in love life, 43, 55, 62, 154, 161
money and, 59, 61
obstacles to, 21
Harmony, 44, 49, 78, 79, 81, 86
Hawking, Stephen, 36
Hay, Louise, 159
Headache, relieving, 67, 92
Healing power
   of crystals/stones, 118, 123, 149, 160
   of marigolds, 82
   of meditation, 150
   psychic power as, 69
   for wounds, 69, 82, 150, 160
The Healing Power of Doing Good, 165
Heart disease, 71, 91, 97
Heart, healing, 160
Heart lines, 164
Heart, opening, 91
Heart, strengthening, 80
Heartbeat, aligning, 78
Help, seeking, 39, 140
Herbs
   benefits of, 26, 42, 68, 80, 158
   ginger, 68
   ginseng, 26
   hawthorn, 80
   Martian qualities, 158
   peppermint, 42
   spicy herbs, 68, 158
Hibiscus tea, 70
Hippocrates, 88
Hobbies, 58
Home/business, decorating, 125, 126
Home/business, protecting, 119, 134
Honesty, practicing, 50

I Ching, 132
Immune system, boosting, 94, 106, 111, 112
Insight, gaining, 63, 140, 151, 154
Inspiration, receiving, 166
Intentions, setting, 121, 137
Intimacy, enhancing, 43, 55, 161
Intuition, increasing, 63, 131, 148, 151, 153

Jackson, Carole, 37
Journals, 16, 41
Joy, 118, 124, 138. *See also* Happiness
Jung, Carl, 81

Kato, Gen, 40
Kindness, 19, 40, 55, 165
Kinesiology, 93
Koan puzzles, 63

Laughter/smiles, 124, 138, 155
Lavender, 28
Law of Attraction, 53, 124
Life
    balance in, 86, 88
    blessing, 156, 163
    enjoying to fullest, 136
    opportunities in, 22, 32, 35, 45, 52
    power days in, 136
    quality of, 18, 25, 40, 103, 107
    sweetness in, 124
Life force, 96
Lotus flower, 148
Love life, 43, 55, 62, 154, 161
Love notes, 33
Love poems, 33, 48
Luks, Allan, 165

Making a Good Brain Great, 58
Mandala, making, 49
Marigolds, 82
Mars, energy of, 158
Massage, 81, 99, 108
Material possessions, 51, 59
Meditation
    with crystals/stones, 123
    healing power of, 150
    mudras and, 29
    for spiritual sharing, 129
    tarot and, 130, 152
Memory, improving, 48, 59, 67, 150
Mercury, position of, 144
Mind
    balancing, 26, 44, 49
    breathing techniques for, 44
    clearing, 32
    exercising, 24, 35, 58, 63, 131
    improving, 24, 42, 48, 58, 131
    playful mind, 138
    power of, 137
    refreshing, 42
    restless mind, 20
    self-care activities for, 13–63
    soothing, 131
    stilling, 20
Mind & Body Health Handbook, 75
Mission statement, 17
Money, 59, 61
Mood, improving, 14, 47, 54, 94, 102. *See also* Happiness
Mudras, 29
Multitasking, ceasing, 18
Music/singing, 38, 106

Neck rolls, 98
Needs, determining, 60, 93

Negativity
impact of, 41
protection against, 119
releasing, 16, 123
tracking, 16
turning into positives, 22
Nonviolence, 133
Nuts, 97

Offerings, making, 121
Online courses, 35, 45, 113
Opportunities, finding, 22, 32, 35, 45, 52
Ornstein, Robert, 75

Pain, easing, 67, 92, 99, 103, 112, 159
Partner, 33, 43, 55, 150, 154, 160, 161, 164
Patterns, changing, 60, 76. *See also* Routines
Peace, finding, 71, 118, 137, 156
Pendulum, 122
Peppermint oil, 42
Peridot, 123
Plastic containers, 101
Poetry, 31, 33, 48
Positive thoughts
benefits of, 41, 118
envisioning, 147
for happiness, 41
positive energy, 137, 147, 165
positive outcomes, 22, 41, 42
power of three, 125
refreshing thoughts, 42
Possessions, 51, 59
Posture, improving, 73, 95
Power
expressing, 143

healing power, 69, 82, 118, 123, 149, 150, 160
power days, 136
power of three, 125
psychic power, 69, 146
Present, focus on, 57, 132
Priorities, 15, 20, 23, 32, 39, 51
Produce, healthy, 79, 110, 114
Prosperity, 59, 121, 127
Psychic power, 69, 146
Purchases, 47, 51, 133
Puzzles, koan, 63

Qualities
desired qualities, 55
of life, 18, 25, 40, 103, 107
Martian qualities, 158
in partner, 55
Quartz, 118, 142

Reflexology, 108
Reich, Wilhelm, 81
Relationships
end of, 160
with family, 39, 112, 124, 129
with friends, 25, 39, 62, 112, 124, 156, 160
intimacy in, 43, 55, 161
love life, 43, 55, 62, 154, 161
with partner, 33, 43, 55, 150, 154, 160, 161, 164
with self, 20, 156
social relationships and, 25
strengthening, 20, 150, 156
Rescue Remedy, 92
Rituals, 99, 142, 167
Rolf, Ida, 81
Rolfing therapy, 81
Rose quartz, 118

Routes, new, 71, 76, 89, 122
Routines, changing
daily routines, 105
new exercises, 100, 113
new explorations, 89
new foods, 84
new hobbies, 58
new routes, 71, 76, 89, 122
new schedules, 60
redecorating, 126
Rowling, J. K., 52
Ruby, 160
Rumi, 48
Runes, 157

Sagan, Carl, 36
Scents
aromatherapy, 28, 102
cedar oil, 99
essential oils, 28, 42, 102, 145
grapefruit oil, 145
lavender, 28
for misting car, 28
peppermint oil, 28
for refreshing thoughts, 42
soaps, 102
Schedule, breaking up, 60
Self-care activities
for body, 65–115
for mind, 13–63
for spirit, 117–67
Self-confidence, 37, 45, 80, 95, 143, 156, 158
Self-deprecation, 66
Self-image, 32, 45, 95
Self-observation, 87
Self-protection, 134
Self-worth, 66

Sex life, 43, 55, 161. *See also* Love life
Sign, sun, 162
Signs, observing, 128
Skin
exfoliating, 77
improving, 74, 77, 99, 147
rejuvenating, 147
soothing, 90
Smiles/laughter, 124, 138, 155
Soap, scented, 102
Sobel, David, 75
Social clubs, 25
Spirit
boosting, 118, 120, 125, 138, 145
deities and, 121, 142, 163
offerings to, 121
self-care activities for, 117–67
soul and, 156
spirit animals, 140
Spiritual growth, 120, 131, 163
Spiritual rituals, 99, 142, 167
Spiritual sharing, 129
Spiritual signs, 128
Spiritual strength, 152
Spiritual teachers, 132, 138
Spiritual thank-you notes, 121
Stamina, boosting, 72
Star gazing, 36
Starting over, 122
Stomach upset, easing, 68, 90
Strength, building, 72, 73, 152
Stress
affecting decisions, 14
calming, 19, 26, 38, 56, 71, 96, 106, 112, 154
computer stress, 67, 98, 149
multitasking and, 18
reducing, 14, 18, 19, 26, 27, 28, 34, 48, 75

relieving, 46, 67, 92, 98, 100, 123, 149, 155, 163
    vacuuming away, 46
Sun sign, 162
Sweetness, sharing, 124
Symbols
    amulets, 119
    charms, 156
    choosing, 135
    colors, 37, 54, 62
    lotus flower, 148
    mandala, 49
    observing, 128
    roses, 62
    runes, 157
    stars, 36
    talisman, 156
    tarot and, 125, 130, 152, 161
    touchstones, 135

Tai chi, 96
Talents, nourishing, 21. *See also* Creativity
Talisman, making, 156
Tarot, 125, 130, 152, 161
Tastes, savoring, 66, 84
Teas
    caffeine-free tea, 70
    ginger tea, 68
    ginseng tea, 26
    hawthorn tea, 80
    hibiscus tea, 70
Tension, easing, 67, 98, 115, 155
Third eye chakra, 75, 151
Topaz, 143
Touch, physical, 112
Touchstone, 135
Tourmaline crystal, 149
Toxins, 29, 101

Trash, picking up, 107
Travel altar, 142
Truth, telling, 50
Twists, doing, 115

Vegetables, 79, 110, 114
Ventilation, 111
Vitamins, 74, 110, 145
Vocabulary, improving, 24, 57

Walks, taking, 71, 76, 86, 109
Water, imprinting, 137
Water, soothing, 56
Wind chimes, 131
Windows, opening, 111
Wish book, starting, 52
Wounds, healing, 69, 82, 150, 160

Yin and yang, 88
Yoga
    breath work for, 85, 111
    dharana, 20
    Fish Pose, 91
    practicing, 20, 29
    routine for, 100
    Warrior Pose, 73
You Can Heal Your Life, 159

Zen koan puzzles, 63
Zoisite, 160

make TIME FOR you!

PICK UP OR DOWNLOAD YOUR COPIES TODAY!